RAISING SUPERSTAR KIDS WITH ADHD

PRACTICAL KNOWLEDGE AND PARENTING TECHNIQUES TO TRANSFORM YOUR EXPLOSIVE CHILD NOW

LYDIA FIELDS

© **Copyright 2022 - All rights reserved.**

The content contained within this book may not be reproduced, duplicated, or transmitted without direct written permission from the author or the publisher.

Under no circumstances will any blame or legal responsibility be held against the publisher, or author, for any damages, reparation, or monetary loss due to the information contained within this book, either directly or indirectly.

Legal Notice:

This book is copyright protected. It is only for personal use. You cannot amend, distribute, sell, use, quote or paraphrase any part, or the content within this book, without the consent of the author or publisher.

Disclaimer Notice:

Please note the information contained within this document is for educational and entertainment purposes only. All effort has been executed to present accurate, up-to-date, reliable, complete information. No warranties of any kind are declared or implied. Readers acknowledge that the author is not engaged in the rendering of legal, financial, medical or professional advice. The content within this book has been derived from various sources. Please consult a licensed professional before attempting any techniques outlined in this book.

By reading this document, the reader agrees that under no circumstances is the author responsible for any losses, direct or indirect, that are incurred as a result of the use of the information contained within this document, including, but not limited to, errors, omissions, or inaccuracies.

CONTENTS

Preface — 7
Introduction — 9

1. THE ADHD BRAIN — 19
   Explaining ADHD — 20
   Causes of ADHD — 21
   Types of ADHD — 22
   The Symptoms of ADHD in Children — 24
   The Neurotypical Brain vs. ADHD — 26
   Summary — 31

2. ADHD DIAGNOSIS — 35
   How is ADHD Diagnosed? — 37
   Conditions Commonly Mistaken for ADHD — 42
   ADHD Child Self-Assessment Test — 50
   Summary — 61

3. ACCEPTANCE IS KEY — 63
   Importance of Acceptance and Awareness — 65
   ADHD Superpowers — 71
   Famous People With ADHD — 76
   ADHD in the Workplace — 79
   A Story of Acceptance — 80
   Summary — 83

4. TREATMENTS FOR ADHD — 85
   Treatment — 87
   Pharmacological Treatments — 88
   Non-Pharmacological Treatments — 93
   Summary — 99

5. BEHAVIORAL THERAPY ... 103
   What Is Behavioral Therapy? ... 105
   Types of Behavioral Therapy ... 105
   Behavioral Therapy Techniques ... 107
   Effectiveness of Behavioral Therapy ... 108
   Children and Behavioral Therapy ... 109
   Finding a Behavioral Therapist ... 109
   Behavioral Parent Training for ADHD ... 110
   Summary ... 116

6. MANAGING INTENSE EMOTIONS ... 121
   Emotions and ADHD ... 124
   Teaching Your Child Emotional Regulation Skills ... 127
   Three Prosocial Emotions for Emotional Regulation ... 130
   The Frustration Log ... 135
   Mindfulness Exercises for Children with ADHD ... 136
   Summary ... 138

7. MAKING FRIENDS ... 141
   ADHD and Your Child's Social Development ... 142
   Improving Your Child's Social Skills ... 143
   How to Make Friends ... 145
   I Say, You Say ... 148
   Summary ... 149

8. GOING TO SCHOOL WITH ADHD ... 151
   ADHD and the Classroom ... 153
   Setting Up Your Child for Success at School ... 154
   School Strategies ... 161
   Summary ... 162

9. DAILY ROUTINES ... 165
   ADHD, Schedules, and Structure ... 167
   Creating ADHD-Friendly Routines ... 168
   Being Strict but Flexible ... 170
   Providing Discipline for Your Misbehaving Child ... 171
   Taking a Deeper Look at Routines and ADHD ... 174
   Routines for Your Child ... 174
   Sample Schedule ... 176
   Summary ... 177

Conclusion ... 181
Glossary ... 189
Bibliography ... 197

Content warning: Chapter 4's "Non-Stimulant Medications" section contains some discussion of suicidal thoughts, substance abuse, and addiction. Readers who may be unsettled by these topics should proceed with caution. Alternatively, this section may be skipped; doing so will not hinder your enjoyment of or takeaways from the book.

INTRODUCTION

Everybody is a genius. But if you judge a fish by its ability to climb a tree, it will live its whole life believing that it is stupid.

— UNKNOWN

I will never forget the pain felt by the entire community. A teacher who had worked for the school from its inception, who everyone loved and respected, did something unthinkable. She had been kind enough to offer to transport children whose parents were struggling to and from school with her. The children loved her, and she loved them, but there was one student she had challenges with. He did not act the same as the other students. She could not get through to him, no matter what she tried. One day, she reached the end of her rope. She brought him to school, left him in the car, and told him to think about his behavior. The teacher then went along with her day. The student could not. It was hours before they found the four-year-old unconscious and barely breathing. He died in the hospital.

I remember the shock I felt at learning what had taken place, worse when it was revealed that the student had displayed special needs tendencies. He had been trying as best he could, but his brain did not always cooperate with him. I remember thinking that what had occurred was more than just negligence; it was a complete lack of understanding of the child and the thoughts that governed his behavior.

When my child was diagnosed with Attention Deficit Hyperactive Disorder (ADHD), my entire world changed. Daily life was challenging and often frustrating. However, one thought always kept me going: if I wanted my child to live a happy, fulfilling life, I needed to do my best to understand her. I was determined that, despite the hard days, the bills, and the worry, my child and I were in this together, and so I began my research. It is this information, and this journey, that I would like to share with you.

First, you are not alone. An examination of 175 research studies across the globe showed that out of 1.7 billion people aged 5–19, 129 million have been diagnosed with ADHD (CHADD, n.d.). All these families face the same things you do. All of you have beautiful, amazing kids who struggle with ADHD. All these families must find ways to cope and provide for their children in the best way possible. You are not alone in this. There is a community, and we are here for you.

You worry about your child's future. You ask yourself: will they survive and thrive out in the world? How will they cope as adults? Will they be able to stand on their own without me? You spend your time analyzing your actions, wondering if you have done enough to set them on the right path for life. The worst days are the ones where the money just simply isn't enough. You cannot afford the treatments and therapies they need. Your only alternative is to do your own research online and from books. Yet despite all your research, despite all the information online, direct approaches and techniques are relatively hard to find. Programs and support for children with ADHD and their families are not easily accessible. The information is so scattered that you spend days putting it all together so you can try whatever you can to help your child. But the things you have researched do not always work. So you go back and begin all over again.

During all this, the bills mount up, and your other children struggle because they feel neglected. Your professional life becomes affected. And you are angry. You love your child so much that their suffering is your own. All you want is for them to be happy. You know the pain and discrimination they may face in the world. You do everything you can to make your family a warm, loving, and safe space for every member.

It is hard, painful, and frustrating. But it is not something you have to go through alone.

In reading this book, you will come to understand your child better and become equipped with tools to help them reach their full potential. This is a step-by-step guide that focuses on the developmental needs of your child as they grow. The steps provided are direct, up-to-date, and have been proven effective in raising well-adjusted and successful children with ADHD. You will gain a greater understanding of the disorder and your child, and learn how to foster better relationships with them.

This book is more than a record of children with ADHD and how their parents can aid them. It is my story, my struggle. It is everything I have learned in trying to be the best mother possible to my daughter.

My sweet baby girl was always active, always asking "why". Her enthusiasm was infectious, if somewhat exhausting. At first, I thought that school would satisfy her curiosity and help her to direct her energy. By the fourth daycare, I began to wonder. The teachers all complained that she could not sit still and did not play well with her classmates. Her activities remained unfinished, and all she wanted to do was play. One by one, I received regretful calls from principals informing me that my child was "just not the right fit for their school." Oftentimes, my husband or I had to leave work to pick her up early. We tried babysitters, but they too soon made their excuses and left. Our families tried to support us as best they could, but they had their own lives.

My daughter was not oblivious to what was happening. We had tried several times to get her to behave the way we wanted her to. Her teachers had done the same. At first, I thought she was just defiant. Slowly I began to realize that my daughter was trying her hardest. She was so empathic that she saw my stress and worry and wanted to help. Her classmates did not want to play with her, and her teachers isolated her in an effort to manage her behavior. People started calling her 'rude' and 'bad.' Soon, she began to believe them. It hurt her, and when I saw how troubled all this made her, it broke my heart. My child was not 'bad'; my child needed help.

When she was six, I took her to be tested for ADHD. The doctor revealed that she did indeed have ADHD, and my world crumbled. Back then, all I knew was that children with this disorder were rambunctious and had limited self-control. I had heard of teachers who refused to have these children in their classrooms. The parents of children with ADHD, it was said, took the easy way out and drugged their children. Look at the criminal system, some said, see how many people with ADHD end up in jail. I was terrified for my child's future but had hope that now that doctors knew more about her condition, things would start getting better.

The reality was that the diagnosis was just the beginning. Many doctors prescribed medication, checked that the medication worked, and left it at that. Interventions and programs for children with ADHD were hard to find. I spent hours on the internet doing so much research. I learned about tools and strategies that could help. I learned more about the stigma and challenges my child would face in the future. Fast forward nine years and my daughter is flourishing. Her thoughts are her own, and her academic performance is outstanding. The journey was hard physically, emotionally, and financially, but seeing her go through life with her head held high made it all worth it.

One of the key strategies I learned is cognitive behavioral therapy, which I will share with you in detail in this book. This strategy helped my child and me to understand the connection between feelings, thoughts, and behavior. The process was very active and problem-focused. With this strategy, you will receive a support network that lets you know there are people there for you. Your child will have increased self-esteem and learn how to be more solution-oriented rather than solely focusing on the problem. Your child will be taught to turn the constant negative thoughts into more positive ones.

Behavioral therapy teaches you how to identify, analyze, and understand the reasons behind anger. Your child will learn to focus and direct this anger, as well as how to communicate effectively with others. You will be given tools to cope with ADHD and intense emotions like grief and stressful situations. These tools will also teach your child to self-evaluate and recognize certain signs that signal a relapse. Your child will be able to use what they have learned to change course and stay on the right path.

Reading this book will help you coach your child to be independent and ask for help when they need it. If you are unsure if your child has ADHD, this book will help you recognize the signs. Your child has a superstar hidden inside them, and you can learn how to unlock their full potential. ADHD is challenging, but it can be managed. Your child can thrive and be successful.

There are countless stories of children with ADHD who excel in school. They are accepted into prestigious universities and offered scholarships and awards. These are children whose parents believed in them, encouraged them, and took action when they felt something was not right. Many of these children attribute their success to parents who never gave up on them despite the challenges.

Actresses like Zooey Deschanel and Emma Watson have been diagnosed with ADHD. Zooey has used crafts as a way to manage her disorder rather than being medicated. Ryan Gosling and Will Smith also have ADHD. So do Simone Biles and Michael Phelps. In the music industry, stars such as Justin Timberlake, Adam Levine, Will.I.Am, and Solange Knowles have also been diagnosed, as have Agatha Christie, John Lennon, Walt Disney, Mozart, Thomas Edison, Albert

Einstein, Leonardo Da Vinci, and many more. (Cole, 2021). All these people were masters of their craft; celebrities, physicists, writers, composers, and artists. Your child can succeed. With the right tools, your child WILL succeed.

This book will help you get there. You will be given an in-depth look at the diagnosis, shown how to accept ADHD as a part of your life and learn about various treatments. You will be provided with tools to help your child manage their emotions and navigate social interactions. You will read about strategies to help your child cope at school and establish routines.

As I have said before, this is my story that I am sharing with you. I understand what you are going through, and I stand with you. My daughter is now excelling at school, confident in herself, and sure about her future. The journey to get to this point was not easy. There were a lot of struggles and sleepless nights—a lot of worry and tears. An ADHD diagnosis is life-changing. There are good days and bad days. It was even harder a decade ago when I began my research. The stigma and lack of support made things difficult. Things have improved since then, but it can still be tough. This is why I am sharing everything I have learned with you. I want you to have one less sleepless night and shed one less tear. I want you to hear more than the dispassionate voice of a medical practitioner. My experience is not just my own; it is the experience of 129 million people across the globe. With this book, I want you to know that you are heard. We are a family, and families are there for each other.

1

THE ADHD BRAIN

People sometimes say, "a penny for your thoughts." I remember trying this with my daughter using dimes. Within just a few months, she was rich.

A lot happens in the brain of a child diagnosed with ADHD, and it can be difficult for you as the parent to understand. This chapter will aid you in doing so. You will learn about symptoms of ADHD, and some key differences between the brain of someone with ADHD and a neurotypical brain. This will save you a fortune in dimes as you grow to understand your child.

A study done by the World Health Organization (WHO) showed that 8.1% of school-aged children in the USA have been diagnosed with ADHD. Norway, Germany, and Spain show estimates of 1.9%, 1.8%, and 5.4%, respectively (ADHD Institute, n.d.). This is not an isolated disorder. Children with ADHD can be found worldwide. Understanding them and providing them with guidance is one of the keys to a better future across the globe.

EXPLAINING ADHD

Attention Deficit Hyperactive Disorder affects how people behave. One in 10 children has been diagnosed with ADHD, and this disorder follows them through childhood and into adulthood. People with ADHD typically display a lack of impulse control, restlessness, and difficulty concentrating. The symptoms of ADHD are observable, especially when the child begins school. As a result, children are typically tested and diagnosed between ages 3–7; however, this is not always the case. Some people don't get diagnosed until well into adulthood. While the symptoms may improve as the person ages, they will always face certain challenges. Anxiety and sleep disorders occasionally come with ADHD.

It is important to note that children are naturally rambunctious and impulsive. This does not necessarily mean they have ADHD. However, you should not ignore any concerns you have. If you believe your child may have ADHD, you can talk to the child's teacher, guidance counselor, and medical professional. They will help you to understand and collect information on your child's behavior in various settings. This will help you to better understand if your child is displaying behavior that is a cause for concern.

CAUSES OF ADHD

The exact cause of ADHD remains unknown. While the source is not fully understood, certain factors are thought to have an impact on whether or not a child will develop ADHD.

The first factor is genetics. Research has shown that ADHD runs in families. It is believed to be a result of complex genetic faults. Research in this area is ongoing as scientists try to find a direct cause. Scientists have also identified several pre- and post-natal causes. These include exposure to substances such as lead, alcohol, and tobacco during pregnancy, premature birth, and low birth weight. Children who receive brain injury during pregnancy or later in life are also at risk.

The structure and function of the brain have also been identified as factors for ADHD. Research is still unclear on this. However, scientists have observed that some parts of the ADHD brain are smaller or larger than those of a neurotypical brain. Some have suggested there is a difference in brain chemistry.

ADHD is thought by many to be the result of sugar, excessive television, and chaotic family life. However, research has not proven any of these claims to be true. It is said instead that these things may make the symptoms worse.

TYPES OF ADHD

I've seen a lot of social media posts and videos saying, "you have ADHD if you…" I have also seen people claiming that "you cannot possibly have ADHD because you don't…" There are many different claims about the disorder, making self-diagnosis confusing. These posts have become increasingly popular. I believe many of these people are trying to help, but there is a downside to a lot of the content being shared. So many people view these posts and say, "Oh, then I must have ADHD because I'm like that." They do this without understanding the disorder and what it means. I have also seen people who are likely to have ADHD say that they do not because they only experience some of the symptoms and end up not getting the help they need. You see, there are three different types of ADHD. As a parent of a child with ADHD, it is important to know these types so you can better understand your child.

Combined ADHD

The first type is the most common. Your child presents all the behaviors associated with ADHD. They are hyperactive, impulsive, and inattentive. Some examples of these behaviors are being overly impatient, active, and too talkative. Your child does sloppy, incomplete work, is easily frustrated, and does not think of the consequences of their actions. They display strong attention-seeking behaviors and typically clown around. They constantly want validation and for people to see and pay attention to them. They often goof off and play around. Some are known as the "class clowns."

Impulsive/Hyperactive ADHD

This is the rarest form of ADHD. With this type, your child is not easily distracted and unfocused. Paying attention is not a major problem for them. They are, however, impulsive and hyperactive. Examples of the behaviors for this type are being restless, always moving, and overly talkative. Your child acts without thinking and does not consider the consequences of their actions.

Inattentive ADHD

With this type, your child is not hyperactive. They display unfocused, inattentive behaviors. These include being messy, disorganized, and easily distracted. Your child seems to constantly be in a fog and needs constant supervision. They daydream a lot and tire easily. They have difficulty completing tasks and tend to lose things. This type is also known as Attention Deficit Disorder (ADD).

THE SYMPTOMS OF ADHD IN CHILDREN

Inattention

Symptoms of inattention that may present themselves in your child are having a short attention span and lacking age-appropriate study skills. Your child has difficulty listening to others and focusing on details. They are easily distracted and constantly switch from one thing to another. If a task does not seem enjoyable to them, they become easily bored within minutes. Their organizational skills are poor, and their work is often incomplete. Your child may seem to be always daydreaming and has trouble following instructions and processing information. They often seem confused and are always losing things.

Impulsivity

Being impulsive is a natural part of being a child. This can make it difficult for you to determine if your child is displaying symptoms of ADHD or if they are simply going through a phase. Your child may be impatient and often acts without thinking. They interrupt others and have trouble waiting for their turn—they are restless during games and will blurt out answers at school without being called on. They want what they want, and they want it now. Your child makes inappropriate comments and does not restrain their emotions. It's very easy to tell how they feel because they will show and tell you without holding back. Your child is also a risk-taker. They do whatever comes to mind without considering consequences.

Hyperactivity

Having a hyperactive child can be exhausting. It is almost impossible to get them to keep still. When you finally think you have them in one place and you can stop and take a breather, off they go. Your child is always in motion, sometimes without direction or purpose other than to move. They are always running and climbing over anything and everything. Keeping them in their seat is next to impossible. Your child is always squirming, fidgeting, turning their heads, and moving their hands and feet. They will grab and manipulate the things around them without thought. Your child has trouble sitting still for meals, stories, and any activity that requires moments of quiet and stillness. They are extremely talkative and forgetful. It is very easy for them to lose things, and they may have difficulties sleeping.

THE NEUROTYPICAL BRAIN VS. ADHD

In conducting my research, I realized that I had to learn some science. I did well enough in the science subjects in school, but the larger terms and theories were intimidating. However, I saw that understanding my daughter meant understanding how her brain works. ADHD is highly researched, and scientists have done an extensive examination of how the ADHD brain differs from the neurotypical brain. These differences help us understand not just the *what* of the behavior but also the *how* and *why*. So with some trepidation, I put on my scientist hat and tried to make sense of what I read.

Neuroscience is essentially the study of the functions and structure of the brain. It examines how the body moves, how senses work, and the formation and expression of memories and emotions. A neurotypical brain behaves and functions in a manner that is considered average for a general population. Anything that strays from that average can result in behavior that is noticeably different from the norm. Your brain is the computer that controls your body and mind.

Knowing the differences in brain performance and the reason behind these differences will go a long way in helping you understand your child.

Let us dive right in with what I found to be a big word: norepinephrine. This is both a stress hormone and a chemical in the body. When you are stressed, the hormone norepinephrine goes into your blood and tells your brain to pay attention. It also increases your heart rate and blood flow. As a chemical, norepinephrine sends signals to your different nerve cells. This communication makes you more focused and quicker to react. Norepinephrine is often associated with dopamine. Dopamine helps control your movements and promotes habits by making you feel pleasure when doing certain things. It also helps you process information and emotion. Not having enough of both chemicals is a factor in ADHD. The neurotypical brain has enough of these chemicals to tell you to focus, react, think, and repeat. The ADHD brain does not get as many of these signals.

Research has also shown functional differences in the four parts of the brain when ADHD is present. These four main parts are the frontal cortex, limbic system, basal ganglia, and reticular activating system.

The parts and structure of the brain and how it functions and develops play a role in how the brain of a child with ADHD works differently from a neurotypical brain.

Brain Structure

▷ **The Frontal Cortex**

The frontal cortex is the part that tells you to pay attention and think about the consequences. Prompts to be alert and try to predict what is happening around you come from the frontal cortex. It also helps you to manage your impulses and emotions. The frontal cortex plays an important role in your decision-making and concentration. A child with ADHD has difficulty regulating what catches their attention. Their frontal cortex is not as active as the norm. As a result, your child constantly switches from task to task. Your child will be doing their homework and come across a math question involving food. This causes their attention to immediately switch to eating, and they go to the kitchen. However, they hear music, which reminds them of a video they like, so they go to watch that video. The thought of homework gets drowned out by each new thought, and they cannot help but respond to whatever idea is the most prominent at the moment.

▷ **The Limbic System**

This system deals with your emotions and behavior. It helps you with storing and retrieving memories. It also helps you with behavior that is necessary for your survival, like eating, fight-or-flight response, reproduction, and caring for your children. It connects your thoughts to your actions. The limbic system of a child with ADHD is overactive. As a result, they are extremely sensitive to sensations, and their brain does not always interpret messages correctly. Your child can become restless or emotionally volatile. You might see something as irritating and react accordingly because that is how your brain interprets what is happening to you. For your child, what might simply be an irritant can be interpreted by their brain in a more exaggerated way, prompting the child to respond by having a complete meltdown.

▷ **The Basal Ganglia**

The basal ganglia control movement. If you decide to move in some way, the basal ganglia help the brain process what you want to do and then carry out the action. Your motivations are influenced by this part of your brain as well. It helps you in choosing behaviors you find to be rewarding, which leads to habit development. The basal ganglia also help with your emotions. For a child with ADHD, this part of the brain is shown to be smaller than average. Deficiencies in the basal ganglia can result in disruption in how the brain communicates. Your child's brain short-circuits, and they become impulsive and inattentive.

▷ The Reticular Activating System

This system acts as a filter. It helps you organize and register information. You are constantly introduced to billions upon billions of stimuli and data from your environment. The reticular activating system helps you process all this data and select what is important. This prevents you from being overloaded by countless sensations. Because of this system, you can choose what to pay attention to and what to tune out. Scientists have observed differences in this system between the ADHD and neurotypical brain. Because of the difference in the way information is filtered, your child may become impulsive and hyperactive.

Brain Function

Your brain has many functions and tasks, most of which are carried out unconsciously. For a child with ADHD, these functions are disrupted. They have difficulty learning from their mistakes, making decisions, and planning events and activities. Paying attention and maintaining focus is difficult for them. Their social skills, organization, memory, motivation, and impulse control are also affected. They also experience challenges with task-switching and hyperactivity.

Your child's emotions, moods, and inter-brain connections and communications all function differently. Parts of their brain are either more hyperactive than the norm or less so. There is, therefore, a challenge in the way their brain responds to stimuli. Your child is not easily able to regulate their brain activity.

Brain Development

Scientists have discovered that the ADHD brain is smaller and takes a longer time to mature. The size, however, does not mean your child is less intelligent. While some parts of the brain take a longer time to mature, the parts dealing with motor skills are found to mature faster than those of the neurotypical brain. The immaturity can lead to a little hitch in the brain that affects how it operates. However, the quickly maturing motor skills explain why your child is restless and always on the move. Because their brain develops slower in certain areas, the way it communicates and relays information is hindered.

SUMMARY

Attention Deficit Hyperactive Disorder follows your child from childhood to adulthood and affects the way they behave. Your child is likely to be hyperactive, impulsive, and have difficulty concentrating. The exact cause is unknown, but it has been linked to genetics as ADHD has been shown to run in families. Other factors include brain injury and exposure to harmful substances during birth or childhood. Being born prematurely or having low weight at birth are also factors.

There are three main types of ADHD. The first and most common is combined ADHD, where your child is hyperactive, impulsive, and inattentive. The second, and rarest type, is impulsive/hyperactive ADHD. With this, your child can focus and pay attention but is restless and acts without thinking. Finally, the third is inattentive ADHD, otherwise called Attention Deficit Disorder (ADD). If your child has ADD, they are not hyperactive. Instead, they daydream a lot and have trouble focusing, planning, and organizing.

There are several differences between the neurotypical brain and the ADHD brain. The ADHD brain is smaller and matures at a different pace. The two chemicals, dopamine and norepinephrine, are lower. The way the frontal cortex, limbic system, basal ganglia, and reticular activating system operate is different. These parts of the brain control and regulate emotion, habits, physical actions, memory, motivation, focus, concentration, and how information is filtered. Because some parts are too active while others are less active than average, there is a challenge in how your child perceives and interprets sensations and information. As a result, your child has difficulties with memory, organization, socialization, and planning. They act without considering the consequences, and their attention is constantly shifting from one thing to another.

Understanding the hows and whys of the ADHD brain will help bring you one step closer to understanding how your child operates. However, the actual diagnosis is determined by a medical professional. The next chapter looks at ADHD diagnosis and treatment.

2

ADHD DIAGNOSIS

The only thing worse than having to do a million and one tests was waiting for the results. However, I could not show my worry and fear in front of my daughter. She wanted to know why she had to go to the doctor so often and do all these tests. Sometimes she got frustrated and did not want to go. After all, people went to the doctor when they were sick, and she felt fine. So why, she would ask, was she going there so much? I didn't know what to tell her. How do I explain the possibility of ADHD to my six-year-old daughter, especially when I didn't know for sure? She was already so insecure and troubled because of how her behavior was perceived by others. Thankfully, the doctors were very kind and considerate. When I confided in them, they did their best to comfort both her and me. I still don't know if I said or did the right things for her in those moments, but we got through all the tests.

Then came the evaluations, and my brain went a mile a minute. If she did not have ADHD, was her impulsiveness, distraction, and hyperactivity simply a result of bad parenting on my part? If so, where did I go wrong, and how could I possibly fix it? How could I have possibly been such a bad parent when I loved my girl so much? I thought to myself that if she was diagnosed with the disorder, then at least I would know there was a reason, an explanation. But then I began thinking that I did not know enough about ADHD. If that was her diagnosis, how would I even begin to help her? What would her future look like? Either option had scary possibilities in my mind. Eventually, the results came in. I looked across at my daughter and knew that she had a long, long road ahead of her. I needed to help her along that road, and I had no clue where to start.

Throughout the evaluation, I was online constantly, trying to learn what I could. I discovered that ADHD was more prevalent in males, who were three times more likely to be diagnosed than females. Research showed that 13% of men were likely to be diagnosed with ADHD, while the percentage for women was 4.2. Most children are diagnosed by age seven, with the symptoms typically appearing between ages 3–6.

HOW IS ADHD DIAGNOSED?

While you may suspect your child has ADHD, the only way to be sure is to do testing. There are many different disorders with symptoms that seem similar to ADHD. There is no singular test, and your healthcare professional will talk not just to you but to other adults your child comes in contact with. These include teachers and other family members. This helps the professional get a full view of how your child behaves in certain settings so that environmental factors can then be ruled out as the major cause of your child's behavior. Your healthcare provider will also examine the symptoms to see if the child may have a different condition or has other conditions along with ADHD. The Diagnostic and Statistical Manual of Mental Disorders (DSM-5) is the gold standard that helps determine whether or not your child has ADHD. The American Psychiatric Association published the fifth edition of this test in 2013. This test is used across the medical field, ensuring that all children are evaluated in the same way. It helps professionals understand the percentage of children with this disorder and its impact on the public.

The DSM-5 provides a list of criteria that the professional uses to assess and diagnose your child.

The DSM-5 Criteria

The DSM-5 assesses your child's attention levels, hyperactivity, and impulsiveness. Your child is likely to have ADHD if they present six or more symptoms of inattention, hyperactivity, and impulsiveness before age 16. For 17 and older, the benchmark is five or more symptoms. These symptoms should be inappropriate based on their level of development and should last more than six months.

Where inattention is concerned, your child is likely to be diagnosed with ADHD if the child:

- is easily and often distracted
- does not do well at organizing activities and tasks
- tends to forget daily activities
- is always losing things, especially those that are used for tasks and activities (eyeglasses, keys, books, cellphones, school materials, wallets)
- dislikes and avoids tasks that require them to think and focus for a long period (for example, schoolwork)
- has challenges with paying attention when completing tasks or engaging in games
- makes careless mistakes and does not pay attention to details

- does not appear to listen when you speak to them directly
- fails to finish chores, homework, and work tasks, and does not follow through on instructions

The symptoms of hyperactivity and impulsiveness should be disruptive to the child's daily life. Your child may have ADHD if the child:

- interrupts others or intrudes in their activities
- is always squirming, tapping their hands or feet, and generally fidgeting
- is constantly talking
- is always moving and going as if operated by a powerful, inexhaustible motor
- has trouble engaging in quiet leisure activities
- runs and climbs even when it is not appropriate to do so (or constantly feel restless if they are in their adolescence)
- has trouble remaining seated and will often get up even when required to stay sitting
- does not wait for a question to be completed before blurting out the answer
- has difficulties waiting for their turn

The DSM-5 also sets out other criteria to be met before a diagnosis of ADHD can be made. Several of the symptoms must present themselves before age 12 and must be present in two or more environments (for example, at home, school, during activities, or socialization). The symptoms must interfere with their daily function and quality of life in the various environments. A diagnosis is given if the symptoms cannot be better explained by other disorders or factors and do not only happen as a result of a psychotic disorder.

The DSM-5 evaluation helps to identify the type of ADHD—listed in the previous chapter—that your child has. Your child's symptoms can change over time, leading to a change in the type of ADHD that they have (CDC, n.d.).

Talking to Your Doctor

If you have concerns that your child might have ADHD, you can discuss this with your general practitioner. They may ask you questions such as:

- What symptoms does your child display?
- When did these symptoms start?
- In what environment do these symptoms present themselves (at school, home, etc.)?
- Does it affect your child's daily life? Does it make socializing difficult?

- Has anything significant happened to your child recently? Has there been a divorce or death in the family?
- Does your family have a history of ADHD?
- What other health conditions does your child have?

If your doctor believes your child could have ADHD, they will suggest observing your child for around ten weeks to see if and how the symptoms change. They will offer training and suggest groups and programs for parents with children who have ADHD. This is intended to help you better understand your child and to provide you with the tools and strategies to help them manage their behavior. If it is seen that these symptoms are getting worse and affect your child's daily life, your doctor will refer you to a specialist who will conduct a formal assessment.

The type of specialist depends on who is in your area, so you may be referred to a psychiatrist, pediatrician, or any qualified health professional with expertise in diagnosing ADHD. The assessment includes a physical examination, multiple interviews with you and your child, and interviews of other adults who interact with your child regularly.

CONDITIONS COMMONLY MISTAKEN FOR ADHD

ADHD-like symptoms can present themselves in several other disorders or as a result of other situations. As a result, a misdiagnosis can happen. Your child might enter school a bit younger than their classmates and therefore be at a different developmental level. Their behavior in school reflects this level and can be mistaken for ADHD symptoms. Hyperactivity and lack of focus and attention are also a normal part of being a child. Boys are also more likely to be diagnosed than girls. Research has shown that girls are more likely to be inattentive than boys, who tend to be more hyperactive. As hyperactivity is more noticeable, boys tend to be diagnosed more often.

Mood Disorders

▷ **Depression**

While depression and ADHD can occur at the same time, it is also possible to confuse the former with the latter. Both have symptoms of mood swings, lack of focus, and forgetfulness. However, ADHD moods are influenced by something occurring that causes a setback, while depressive moods are more constant. While people with depression may fall asleep and wake several times during the night, people with ADHD have trouble falling asleep in the first place. People with depression typically have little interest in beginning an activity, whereas those with ADHD have difficulty choosing which activity to do. Children who suffer from depression tend to exhibit symptoms similar to those experienced by adults.

▷ **Bipolar Disorder**

People with bipolar disorder experience alternating moments of heightened emotion and depression. The high moments are called the manic stage, in which an individual may talk a lot and switch from topic to topic. They may also take risks and have trouble sleeping. This can be mistaken for hyperactivity. The lack of attention and motivation during the low moments are also considered to be similar to symptoms of ADHD. However, bipolar disorder creates a greater disruption in the person's life, and the symptoms develop over time. A child with bipolar disorder will rage and be more destructive than a child with ADHD. Tantrums will also carry on for longer, as they are not as easily distracted or exhausted from their rage as a child with ADHD. A child with bipolar may also display violent behavior toward animals, hallucinate, and have disturbing nightmares.

▷ **Dysthymia**

Dysthymia is depression that is mild but persistent. People with dysthymia have low self-esteem, a lack of energy, and are generally irritable. Your child might have dysthymia if they under- or overeat, are easily fatigued, have problems with concentration and making decisions, sleep too much or too little, have low self-esteem, and feel hopeless. These symptoms must present themselves for over a year. The symptoms of dysthymia are sometimes mistaken for ADHD. Your child can develop dysthymia as a result of having ADHD.

Auditory Processing Disorder (APD)

People with APD experience challenges with understanding sounds, including speech. APD can sometimes be mistaken for ADHD as children with ADHD often have problems focusing on and processing sensations such as sound. Because of the trouble understanding sounds, children with APD can be seen as lacking focus and attention. The children will also react to their problems with sensory input in a way that may lead people to believe they have ADHD. It is possible to identify which disorder your child has by observing their interaction with sound-related tasks and comparing it with how they complete non-auditory tasks. If your child does not do well with listening but performs well with reading, they may have APD, whereas a child with ADHD is likely to display a lack of focus across multiple tasks. It is also possible for a child to have both APD and ADHD.

Allergies

Allergies can be quite irritating for children, and they may not always be able to adequately express what they are feeling. They may become irritable and unfocused as a result of their discomfort. Allergy symptoms can also cause them to be fatigued and have difficulty sleeping. While at school, the child might fidget and fail to complete tasks. As a result, allergies can sometimes be misdiagnosed as ADHD. You can evaluate if your child has allergies or ADHD by observing their symptoms and duration. These symptoms might be seasonal and reflect those commonly experienced by persons with allergies.

Visual Problems

If your child has vision problems, they may seem to lack focus and attention. The effort required to focus on the world around them may also affect how they behave. They may be easily exhausted, forgetful, and have trouble with organization. Visual problems can also make it difficult for your child to complete tasks and schoolwork. Their visual challenge may make them frustrated and irritable, and they may have outbursts. If you believe your child has been misdiagnosed, you can take them to have their eyes tested.

Obsessive-Compulsive Disorder (OCD)

A person with obsessive-compulsive disorder is plagued by constant, uncontrolled thoughts that cause them distress. In reaction to this distress, the person completes tasks to bring order to their thoughts and feelings. Both ADHD and OCD can affect a person's attention and focus, as well as cause them to experience and express intense emotions. However, a person with OCD tends to follow consistent patterns and rituals. They are more likely to focus on details than a person with ADHD.

Anxiety Disorders

Anxiety disorders may cause your child to feel distressed and uneasy in situations that may seem calm and normal to you. These feelings of anxiety can become so severe that they affect your child's ability to function in daily life. Your child may be restless and have trouble with concentration and attention. You may interpret these symptoms as being the result of possible ADHD. You can observe your child in multiple situations and evaluate if they are restless and lack attention in cases where they feel nervous or if they have difficulty focusing and paying attention regardless of the situation.

Autism Spectrum Disorder (ASD)

Autism spectrum disorder affects a person's brain, nerves, and development, influencing how they communicate, behave, and learn. This disorder is on a spectrum because there are many variations in the type and symptoms. ASD and ADHD can be confused in early stages due to similar difficulty with concentration and communication. There are several ways to differentiate between the two. For example, a child with ASD may have slow or no speech development and avoid eye contact and social situations.

Oppositional Defiant Disorder (ODD)

Children with oppositional defiant disorder will deliberately disobey rules, argue with anyone they perceive to be an authority figure, say mean things, and constantly lose their temper. These things happen naturally as a part of a child growing up. However, once they have passed toddlerhood and are advancing through childhood, this behavior becomes a cause for concern. The symptoms of ODD are sometimes confused with those of ADHD. While children with ADHD are restless and distracted, children with ODD are angry and defiant.

Conduct Disorder (CD)

Children with conduct disorder tend to break the rules, which can escalate to the point that their actions might be criminal. They show little regard for possessions, property, and people. They may steal from and threaten those around them. The lack of impulse control and socialization problems sometimes cause conduct disorder to be confused with ADHD. It is possible for a child with ADHD to develop CD, but both disorders have distinct symptoms.

Learning Disabilities

Having a learning disability makes it difficult for a person to process and understand information. Learning disabilities can affect speech, reading, movement, perception, and more. As a result, your child may be distracted during learning, which can cause them to have outbursts due to frustration. Learning disabilities are often confused with ADHD.

Sensory Processing Disorder

Children with sensory processing disorder have difficulty with light, sounds, touch, scent, and anything to do with the five senses. Their brain does not process these sensations in the way the average brain does. They are extremely sensitive and have very strong reactions to stimuli. This response may produce symptoms that are similar to those of ADHD.

Seizure Disorders

A type of seizure called absence seizure may appear to be a symptom of ADHD. In this case, the seizure happens very quickly, and the person may appear to simply blank out and stare into space before once again being alert. This is similar to the symptoms of inattentiveness present with ADHD. However, you can regain a child with ADHD's attention by touching them or making a noise. This will have no effect on someone experiencing an absence seizure.

Tourette's Syndrome

With Tourette's syndrome, people will make involuntary sounds and movements called tics. Some tics a child with Tourette's syndrome might display are jerking limbs, eye blinks and rolls, shrugging, grimacing, twirling, jumping, and touching objects and people. They may also repeat sounds, say random words, grunt, whistle, make animal noises, clear their throat, and click their tongue. These tics can become stronger during moments of stress, fatigue, and anxiety. The movements caused by Tourette's syndrome are sometimes misinterpreted as being restless and hyperactive.

Sleep Disorders

Consistent problems with falling and staying asleep can be a symptom of a sleep disorder. As a result, the person is tired and may be unfocused during the day or act aggressively due to sleep deprivation. This is sometimes confused with ADHD.

Substance Abuse

Drugs of various kinds can sometimes fall into the hands of children. Effects of and reactions to these drugs can cause them to display symptoms that may appear to be signs of ADHD. This possibility should be explored if your child begins to show ADHD-like symptoms as a teenager where no symptoms were present during childhood.

ADHD CHILD SELF-ASSESSMENT TEST

If you think your child might have ADHD, it may be helpful to go through a list of questions to see how closely your child's behavior matches ADHD symptoms. The following is a list of questions to consider, selecting the level of frequency for each. Note that this is not an official diagnosis. For an official diagnosis, you must contact a medical professional. This test serves to help you to evaluate your child's behavior and form a closer idea of what they might be experiencing.

1. Does your family have a history of ADHD?

   - Yes
   - No

2. Has your child experienced a significant change in their family and daily life that could affect their behavior?

   - Yes
   - No

3. Does your child display the symptoms that concern you at home, school, and other environments?

   - Only at home
   - Only at school
   - During specific events
   - In multiple environments (home, school, and otherwise)

4. At what age did you first notice these symptoms?

- 2–4
- 4–7
- 7–10
- 10–15
- 18+

5. Does your child have other health conditions that may cause changes in their behavior?

- Yes
- No

6. Does your child experience challenges at home, school, and in daily life due to these symptoms?

- Yes
- No

The questions below look at your child's levels of attention and focus.

7. How often does your child forget things?

- Never
- Sometimes
- Often
- Very Often

8. Is your child easily distracted?

- Never
- Sometimes
- Often
- Very Often

9. Does your child often forget daily activities?

- Never
- Sometimes
- Often
- Very Often

10. Does your child often lose things?

- Never
- Sometimes
- Often
- Very Often

11. Does your child have trouble with organization?

- Never
- Sometimes
- Often
- Very Often

12. Does your child have trouble focusing and paying attention?

- Never
- Sometimes
- Often
- Very Often

13. Is your child prone to making careless mistakes when completing tasks?

- Never
- Sometimes
- Often
- Very Often

14. Does your child have trouble paying attention to details?

- Never
- Sometimes
- Often
- Very Often

15. How often does your child appear to not be listening when spoken to directly?

- Never
- Sometimes
- Often
- Very Often

16. Does your child fail to complete tasks (for example, chores, homework, schoolwork)

- Never
- Sometimes
- Often
- Very Often

17. Does your child have difficulty waiting their turn in conversations and activities?

- Never
- Sometimes
- Often
- Very Often

18. Does your child have a habit of daydreaming and seeming unfocused?

- Never
- Sometimes
- Often
- Very Often

19. Does your child have difficulty following instructions?

- Never
- Sometimes
- Often
- Very Often

The questions below look at how hyperactive and impulsive your child might be.

20. Is your child always interrupting others?

- Never
- Sometimes
- Often
- Very Often

21. Does your child blurt out answers without waiting for the question to be completed?

- Never
- Sometimes
- Often
- Very Often

22. Does your child run and climb during moments and situations that are inappropriate?

- Never
- Sometimes
- Often
- Very Often

23. Does your child have trouble engaging in quiet activities?

- Never
- Sometimes
- Often
- Very Often

24. How often does your child get up and move about in situations where they are required to remain seated?

- Never
- Sometimes
- Often
- Very Often

25. Is your child constantly on the move with seemingly endless energy?

- Never
- Sometimes
- Often
- Very Often

26. Does your child talk rapidly and constantly?

- Never
- Sometimes
- Often
- Very Often

27. Is your child always squirming, fidgeting, and displaying signs of restlessness?

- Never
- Sometimes
- Often
- Very Often

28. Does your child have emotional outbursts and show signs of being unable to cope with stressful situations?

- Never
- Sometimes
- Often
- Very Often

29. How often does your child become quickly frustrated with difficult tasks?

- Never
- Sometimes
- Often
- Very Often

30. Does your child's attention constantly switch from one thing to another?

- Never
- Sometimes
- Often
- Very Often

SUMMARY

Waiting for the official diagnosis for your child can be nerve-wracking. To diagnose your child, a medical professional will conduct a series of tests and interviews. They will speak to you, your child, teachers, and other persons with whom the child has consistent contact in multiple environments. A physical exam will also be done to rule out other causes. The American Psychiatric Association has released the fifth edition of the Diagnostic and Statistical Manual of Mental Disorders (DSM-5). This is the standard that will be used to evaluate your child's symptoms. The DSM-5 asks about your child's ability to focus, pay attention to information, organize and complete tasks, and follow instructions. It also tests how active your child is and how well they remember things. To be diagnosed with ADHD, a child must display six or more symptoms of inattention and hyperactivity before age 16 and five or more symptoms for those 17 and over. Where hyperactivity is concerned, these symptoms should be inappropriate at their age. Your child can be diagnosed with ADHD if the symptoms of inattentiveness and/or hyperactivity and impulsiveness have been occurring for more than six months.

Many other disorders can be mistaken for ADHD, as symptoms may be similar. In some cases, your child might have these disorders in addition to ADHD. However, close observation will reveal the differences and help pinpoint your child's challenge. If you believe your child has been misdiagnosed, you can bring them to a professional for further testing.

Receiving a diagnosis of ADHD is difficult for both you and your child. The road ahead is difficult but can be managed, with many joys and triumphs along the way. One of the major steps on that road is acceptance, which we will explore in the next chapter.

3

ACCEPTANCE IS KEY

I was devastated at my child's diagnosis. It took me a while to realize I did not need to be. During my research, I discovered the possible genetic and prenatal causes of ADHD. I wondered if it was my fault. I convinced myself I could have been a better mother. My child was different because I had done something wrong. I resolved to be the best parent possible, to guide my child to the best of my ability. I would be patient, understanding, and strive to maintain a good attitude. Research became very important to me because I was determined to learn everything I could to help my daughter. On some level, I felt proud of myself. Here I was, starting a new chapter of accepting the diagnosis and making plans to go forward instead of breaking.

Eventually, I realized the flaw in my thinking. There was a difference between accepting that my child had ADHD and accepting that this was who my child was and that it would be okay. I still felt fear, guilt, sadness, and anger. I wanted her to act in ways I thought were best for her rather than accepting who she was. There were moments when I dwelled on what my child could not do instead of what she could. She was amazing at so many things, and I needed to acknowledge that more. It was easy for me to say, "I accept this," when what I needed to do was feel it. I needed to do more than go through the motions.

ADHD is not a disability; it is a different ability.

You sometimes spend so much time wishing your child were normal. Normal is relative. Your child is special. Imagine struggling with your brain because it doesn't always work the way you want it to. Then imagine getting up, facing the day, and taking on all its challenges. Your child does that, and they are rockstars. They see the world differently. To stand out among the 'normal' shows the courage, strength, and determination your child has. Accepting an ADHD diagnosis means accepting how wonderful and strong your child is. Use this to inspire you to never give up the way your child never gives up.

IMPORTANCE OF ACCEPTANCE AND AWARENESS

You have read the term 'neurotypical' as it relates to the average brain. The term that applies to your child is 'neurodivergent.' This means that the function, structure, development, and maturity of their brain differ from what is considered the norm. When you learn that your child is neurodivergent, it's natural to worry. You want what's best for them, and society considers 'normal' to be what is best. Your child is who they are. Accepting that is very important.

It is good that you are striving to learn all you can to help your child. They need you to be there for them. However, evaluating your child is not the only step. You also need to evaluate yourself. What you think and how you feel about the ADHD diagnosis is very important. Consider if you are blaming yourself and trying to convince yourself that nothing is happening with your child.

Stop.

Take a deep breath.

Let it out.

Now ask yourself:

Are there any issues I have that are influencing how I feel about this diagnosis? Am I trying to deny who my child is? Do I feel fear, anger, and guilt whenever I think about the diagnosis? What were/are my thoughts on neurodiversity? How do those thoughts influence how I feel and what I think about my child's diagnosis? Are there any biases I should reflect on? Am I still holding out hope that there has been a mistake, that this is only temporary, and that my child will eventually become normal?

It is okay to feel sadness that the future you imagined for your child may take a different path. This does not mean that the path is bad or that the destination will change. You can acknowledge this sadness. You mustn't deny what you feel.

Understand that it's not about how you feel your child should act. Just because you think they should speak or behave a certain way doesn't mean that that is what will happen. If your child has an outburst, is inattentive, or active during inappropriate moments, saying, "Well, they really shouldn't behave like this; they know better," is just putting blinders on. What they should not do and what they are doing are two different things. So focus on what is happening rather than what you think should be happening. Don't ignore, deny, or fight against the reality in front of you.

When you get unexpected news or when you are feeling sad, frustrated, or guilty, you tend to look at the downsides. That is a perfectly natural part of being a human being. However, you can check yourself when you catch yourself focusing on all the things your child cannot do and how that affects their life. Look instead at what they can do.

Whenever my daughter was around someone new, I made sure I made them aware of her diagnosis and how she might behave. Eventually, I realized I spent too much time telling people, "she will act up if…" and "you'll find that you will have challenges when…" So I began to talk her up more. It was not fair to her for me to talk about only one aspect of her personality. She was so much more than that. I wanted others to see her as more than her diagnosis, so I took note of all the things she loved and was good at. Whenever I spoke about her, I spoke confidently of all the positive things about her. What I said affected how people viewed her, so I made sure to give a fair representation of my beautiful baby girl.

Whenever you feel the need to explain your child's diagnosis, you should consider who you are sharing information with and why. Is it because you feel you need to make excuses and justifications? Do you feel emotionally safe with the person you're sharing information with? If it's about making excuses and you do not feel emotionally safe, consider explaining less. Explanations are best reserved when you are seeking extra support for your child, for example, with a teacher or babysitter. In this case, you can talk about the positives and offer the tools and strategies you have found to be helpful. Otherwise, there is nothing for you to try to justify.

Consider how much time you spend trying to fix all your child's weaknesses. Ask yourself, am I spending enough time acknowledging and building her strengths? If you find more time is spent working on your child's weaknesses rather than their strengths, consider refocusing your energies. Your child listens to you. You help form their opinions of themselves. By focusing on the positive and what they are good at, you are teaching them to do the same.

ADHD Awareness

Raising awareness of all mental disorders and illnesses is very important. Lack of information and stigma can lead to harmful labeling, bias, and bullying. This negative outlook can even affect the medical profession. Not all doctors are well-versed in ADHD. Some can be careless with diagnoses by saying "boys will be boys" or blaming what a female is going through on her size and hormones.

Too many people believe ADHD is "not a real illness" or that "parents are just looking for excuses to drug their children because they don't know how to handle them." Some feel "those with ADHD don't need medication, they're just druggies and attention-seekers" or "ADHD is the result of sugar, television, and medication." Some even insist that "if people tried hard enough, they wouldn't experience ADHD symptoms."

These beliefs are harmful to children with ADHD and their families. They can even lead these children to contemplate self-harm and suicide. Parents resist getting their children the help they need because of the stigma.

Widespread ADHD awareness can change all that. With increased awareness, schools could better identify the symptoms in students who are otherwise labeled as 'bad' or 'slow.' Schools could make arrangements and implement training to promote an inclusive environment that caters to all students. They could educate their students to prevent bullying and foster understanding. More ADHD awareness would also highlight the importance of educators working hand-in-hand with parents and offering them advice when necessary. ADHD awareness could lead to more intervention and support groups being created and more easily accessible. It would help people with ADHD who have trouble accessing their medicine and getting proper insurance. It might also improve the workplace environment. Raising ADHD awareness can help create safe and welcoming environments in all aspects of life.

Parents, teachers, doctors, employers, and others can benefit from learning about the symptoms of ADHD. It would help them better understand and empathize with those with this disorder. This would help prevent misdiagnosis and improve the quality and availability of support, tools, and strategies.

Thankfully, some individuals and organizations are doing all they can to bring awareness of ADHD across the globe. October is ADHD Awareness Month. During this time, organizations such as Children and Adults with ADD (CHADD) and medical groups concerned with mental health spread awareness about ADHD diagnoses, treatment plans, and conditions that tend to accompany ADHD. They also provide tools and advice to parents and others and discuss how ADHD affects communication and relationships. Seminars, webinars, campaigns, workshops, and events are held. A lot of print materials in the form of books, brochures, and posters are also made available. Persons and organizations visit schools and community centers to spread awareness. Some blogs and websites serve to share inspiring and motivating stories about ADHD. They help connect people and families who live with ADHD. This community works to dispel common misconceptions, create an accepting environment where experiences can be shared, and offer tools, strategies, and support.

You can join the initiative to spread ADHD awareness. You can hold fund-raising events such as dinners, auctions, and walks. Social media is a powerful tool where you can create your own hashtags or use popular ones to help spread awareness. You can create blogs and post in forums to share your experiences. You can also ask those you know with ADHD how you can help.

ADHD SUPERPOWERS

There are so many positives to ADHD. Your child truly is a superstar.

Imagination and Creativity

Your child's imagination and creativity are off the charts. My daughter could take a simple spot on the wall and turn it into an entire world with characters, events, and backstories. I tried to make sure I made time for and encouraged her stories. They were signs of a brilliant, constantly working mind. Sometimes we would put aside our devices and use our imaginations to make our own entertainment.

Good Observation and Memory

You may have trouble believing this if your child tends to be unfocused and forget things, but it's true. Your child has an impressive memory and observational skills. My daughter can fire off the most random facts, and it amazes me every time. Once she notices something, she will never forget it down to the smallest detail, no matter how much time has passed. It was her observational tendencies that helped me to slow down and take notice of the scenery in our community. I was able to recapture the wonder I first felt.

Compassion

Your child may not always socialize well with others or think about the consequences of their actions. However, you will find that your child is amazingly compassionate. Their struggles make them very understanding of others. They will often try to help those less fortunate than they are. Where others might ignore or pass an issue by, they will stop and take notice. They are incredibly kind and loving.

Perseverance

Your child has to work so much harder than the average child. And they do, every single day. Your child has to study harder and think more about their actions. Where our brains will naturally fall in line, your child has to be a general, ordering their thoughts. They never give up. Every time your child gets up and faces the day is admirable.

Sense of Humor

Your child knows how to make people laugh. They can cut through tension and relieve stress by being the silly, sweet person they are. It is hard to stay mad around my daughter. She always knows what to say and do to get a laugh out of me, which helps me to relax. Whenever I get too tightly wound, she is always there with a joke that helps me remember not to be so serious all the time. Enjoying life is important, after all.

Acceptance

Your child sees the world differently, and this makes them more accepting of differences. People have quirks and preferences that may be misunderstood, affecting how they are treated. Your child is more willing to examine the reasons behind people's behavior. They can look beyond the surface and accept people for who they are.

High Level of Energy

Your child can keep going when others will stop. I remember deciding it was time for me to be healthier and exercise more. It was tough, and I wanted to give up many times. My daughter's energy kept me going. She motivated me with verbal encouragement and by making it a competition between us. Seeing the way she kept moving helped me to keep moving too. I was in awe of her energy. She always managed to outlast me. Nothing could stop her.

Ability to Multitask

Your child's ability to switch between tasks can help them accomplish a lot of things concurrently. This can be a big advantage when they are older and begin their career. With some honing and discipline, their ability to shift focus from one thing to another will make them dynamic, fast, and efficient.

Firm Morality

Your child is a champion of what is right. They will always try to live according to their values. There were moments when I tried to be sneaky and have a little more fun than I ought to. My daughter never let me get away with it. She dragged me with her down the straight and narrow path.

Enthusiasm for Life

Your child knows how to put on a genuine smile and face the day and its challenges. They live fully in every moment. You might find your child gets excited about everything, which can be contagious. It's hard to look at the negatives with someone bubbling with such joy and fascination for life.

Intense Focus

When your child pays attention to something, they give it their all. They can pinpoint and examine the small details of whatever they're focusing on. There was not a single board game that my daughter did not completely crush me in. A light would switch on once the game started, and she would just dominate everyone she played against. Once she got like that, nothing else mattered. I would take on the challenge of trying to distract her and fail every time.

Spontaneity

It is hard to be bogged down by boredom and routine with your child around. Your child knows how to enjoy themselves and is willing to take risks and try new things. I especially experienced this with food where my daughter was concerned. We tried the wackiest combinations. Some were good, some terrible, but it was always fun. When she got to choose an activity, I never knew where the day would end up. Her spontaneous nature made things very exciting.

FAMOUS PEOPLE WITH ADHD

ADHD changes the way you and your child go through life, but it is by no means a barrier to success. Many, many famous, successful people have or had ADHD.

Famous Historical Figures With ADHD

- Wolfgang Amadeus Mozart—renowned composer of the 18th century
- Walt Disney—founder of the Disney empire and king of animation
- Alexander Graham Bell—inventor of the telephone and gramophone
- Albert Einstein—a physicist who developed the theories of relativity and quantum mechanics
- Thomas Edison—inventor of motion pictures, generation of electric power, sound recording, mass communication, and much more
- Leonardo Da Vinci—artist, sculptor, painter; creator of the Mona Lisa

Famous Athletes With ADHD

- Simone Biles—Olympic gymnast
- Michael Phelps—Olympic swimmer
- Michael Jordan—basketball player
- Terry Bradshaw—American football player
- Karina Smirnoff—professional dancer

Famous Actors With ADHD

- Will Smith—starred in *Fresh Prince of Bel-Air, Men in Black, Aladdin, Bad Boys, Suicide Squad,* and many other movies
- Zooey Deschanel—acted in *New Girl, Trolls, Bridge to Terabithia,* and many others
- Michelle Rodriguez—famous for in *The Fast and the Furious* franchise, *Avatar, Resident Evil,* and more
- Woody Harrelson—performed in *Venom, The Hunger Games, Star Wars,* and others
- Emma Watson—acted in the *Harry Potter* movies, *Beauty and the Beast, Little Women,* and several others
- Ryan Gosling—famous for *The Notebook, La La Land,* and much more
- Jim Carrey—starred in *The Mask, Ace Ventura, Sonic, Bruce Almighty,* and many more

Famous Singers With ADHD

- Solange Knowles—singer and songwriter
- Will.I.Am—singer, rapper, songwriter, and member of the group Black Eyed Peas
- Loyle Carner—hip-hop musician
- John Lennon—musician, singer, songwriter, peace activist, and member of the Beatles
- Adam Levine—singer and musician, lead singer of the group Maroon 5
- Justin Timberlake—singer, actor, and former member of *NSYNC

Famous Authors With ADHD

- Agatha Christie—author of *Murder on the Orient Express* and 65 other books and 14 short stories
- Jules Verne—pioneer of the science fiction genre
- George Bernard Shaw—author of over 100 plays critiquing the education system of his time
- Dav Pilkey—writer and illustrator of the *Captain Underpants* series

And so many more. These people came from different backgrounds, led different lives, and had different careers. They had two things in common: They had ADHD, and they were successful. Many of them helped shape the world as we know it. Their work created legacies that outlived them and that continue to grow and spread. They are a source of inspiration for many people. They had their own personal struggles, but they focused on their strengths and used their superpowers to succeed (Cole, 2021).

ADHD IN THE WORKPLACE

An ADHD diagnosis will never stop your child from excelling in their chosen field. What some see as a barrier, they can use as their strength. Your child's ability to get hyper-focused can help them in any task they set their minds to and improve their performance. Once your child is hyper-focused, they cannot be easily distracted and will produce high-quality work.

Your child's creativity will help them find unique solutions to problems. Their unique perspective enables them to think outside the box. Your child is resilient, which will help them face challenges and disappointments head-on. They can overcome the setbacks they will face at work.

The high energy your child displays will keep them going at work long after their colleagues have slowed down. This is especially helpful in jobs that require a lot of physical activity. Your child is also a great conversationalist and very empathic and accepting. These traits will aid them with interpersonal relationships at work. Your child is not afraid to live in the moment, enjoy life, and take risks. They are courageous and create lasting, memorable moments in their daily life.

A STORY OF ACCEPTANCE

During my research, I connected with many parents and people with ADHD. I was able to share my experiences and learn from the experiences of others. This touching story of acceptance was one I just had to share with you.

> *"I always wanted a child and knew I would be the perfect mother. I knew just how I would raise my children and the type of people they would be. Whenever I went to the store or passed the playground, I would raise my eyebrows at children having meltdowns or misbehaving. Clearly, they had no proper guidance; otherwise, they would not be acting this way. I wondered where the parents were and why they were not doing anything. There are so many ways to discipline a child, after all. My child, I decided, would be different.*

When my son turned four, I realized I was right. My child was different. He had tantrums, was constantly running around the house, and could never pay attention. As he grew older, it became even more apparent that this was not simply a case of a child being a child. Eventually, he was diagnosed with ADHD, and I said goodbye to all my lofty dreams. My son played rough and took risks that gave me more gray hairs than anything else. Sometimes he seemed to never listen to a word I said, and getting him to complete anything was next to impossible. He was practically attached to my hip because few people wanted to stay with him very long. He had very few friends and frustrated a lot of teachers.

I loved every bit of him. He was so creative and full of life. My son made me laugh like no one else. We faced and overcame many challenges together. He was my inspiration and motivation. He was sweet, kind, and thoughtful.

There were days when I got exhausted and frustrated. Sometimes it felt like I was just not doing anything right as a parent. I had to do so much research and go to so many appointments. My fierce mother bear mode was constantly on, and I was always on the lookout for anyone bullying or discriminating against him. Being the mother of a child with ADHD took so much effort, time, and research. Sometimes it felt like he did not appreciate my efforts at all.

I met others who were going through the same thing. Parents who felt guilty that they were medicating their child. They also felt like they were neglecting their other children because of the attention their child with ADHD needed. People judge them and their children. They are forever on a campaign to ensure their child has the love and support they need from others.

None of this stopped them from loving their children with all their hearts. None of this stopped me from loving mine. My dreams are not the same as they once were, but it doesn't matter. The journey I have been on with my child has been incredible. We have both grown so much and learned about each other. I see the results of my efforts reflected on his face every time he smiles. It is rare, but on occasions, he says, "I love you, Mom," or "thank you," and those moments make my day.

For all those parents who have children with ADHD, I know it can be difficult. But it is worth it. Accepting your child and acknowledging their weaknesses and strengths make both you and them better people. One day they will step out into the world as superstars.

Your child is amazing. By understanding them and loving them with all your heart, you are amazing too."
—M.

SUMMARY

It is important to accept your child for who they are. You should acknowledge their challenges and their strengths. Raising a child with ADHD is not easy. You struggle with feelings of guilt and inadequacy. You worry about your child's future. It's okay to worry and feel sad that your child's road in life will be different. Stop and take some time to self-reflect. Ask yourself how your personal experiences, hopes, and biases influence how you feel about your child's diagnosis. Understand you cannot change your child and you should not try to deny reality. Focus on the positives. Yes, your child has struggles, but talk about their strengths to yourself, to them, and to others. What you say influences how they are viewed by other people.

Your child has superpowers. Their diagnosis gives them advantages in certain areas. They are kind, compassionate, imaginative, creative, persistent, resilient, empathic, full of energy, hyper-focused, spontaneous, humorous, and so much more. Helping them harness these gifts will help them become successful in their lives.

There are many famous historical figures, athletes, actors, singers, and authors with ADHD. All these people successfully used their abilities to climb to the top of their field. They created legacies and built business empires. They created works of art that have inspired generations. ADHD has its difficulties, but it has its blessings too.

As a parent, accepting all of your child is a step toward helping them become the best versions of themselves. You can help others too. Organizations spread ADHD awareness through brochures, seminars, websites, and other activities and events. You, too, can spread awareness by organizing events and sharing your stories. Every effort counts. You can help raise empathy and understanding, promote inclusion in schools, create intervention and support programs, and promote ADHD-friendly health care.

Remember, your child is a superstar, and your love and efforts are not in vain. It can be challenging, but it is okay to ask for help. In the next chapter, we will look at some treatments for ADHD.

4

TREATMENTS FOR ADHD

After receiving the ADHD diagnosis, I had to decide what to do. A part of me wanted to just go on as if nothing had happened. If I held my head under the sand long enough, all the challenges would disappear. But it had happened, and I needed to face it. With some research, I found that there were several options. I could try therapy, medication, meditation, exercise, diet changes, and so much more. All the options were overwhelming, and the stigma attached to them made things even worse. It felt like any choice I made would be the wrong one. I sucked as a parent. My child needed more of me than I could possibly give. Knowing the financial cost attached to some of these treatments provided another thing for me to worry about.

How could I possibly afford this? Was I drugging my child if I chose to medicate? Yet if I didn't, was I withholding something my child desperately needed? How reliable were these methods, anyway? Besides, if my daughter had all these superpowers, should I really try to do something about this disorder? These thoughts and more went round and round in my mind, and I didn't even know where to begin.

Eventually, I stopped reeling and centered myself. I focused on my daughter. She was wonderful. She had all these unique gifts. However, she also had these challenges, and it was up to me as her mother to help her. ADHD has no cure, but it is highly treatable. The symptoms can be managed long-term and are also prone to shift as time passes. With proper treatment and care, my daughter could learn to adjust. But getting that treatment relied on me having a level head and carefully going through all the options.

None of the treatments was a miracle, instant cure-all. It took a lot of time and effort. Some things worked; others did not. What worked for someone else did not always work for my daughter. There was a lot of trial and error, and at times I would get discouraged. I did not let that stop me. I combined both the natural and medical treatments after extensive research and medical consultations and saw amazing improvement. I still and always will worry about my daughter, but I know that she will be okay.

TREATMENT

So your child has ADHD—now what? First, you must explore and consider all the treatment options and decide which one is best for your child and your family. This should not be done alone. Talk to your healthcare professional, your family, your child's teachers, therapists, and anyone else you feel you should be included in the conversation.

Medication

The American Academy of Pediatrics (AAP) recommends medication as a last resort for children under six. For those over six, two types of FDA-approved medications are stimulants and non-stimulants. Medications help manage your child's symptoms, which can improve how they behave and interact with others at home, school, and other environments. These medications may have various side effects, and the dosage takes careful consideration. Each person reacts differently, so the medication that works for one person at a certain dosage may not work for another person in the same way. It's important to work with your healthcare provider and talk with your child to determine if the medication is working. Changes in the medication type or dosage may be necessary.

Behavioral Therapy

Behavioral therapy can be very beneficial, as it teaches your child how to manage their behaviors. Your child learns to reduce negative behaviors and increase positive ones. This type of therapy is often done alongside medication. It is especially recommended for children under six before they are given any medication. The therapy covers many areas and seeks to not only teach the child but parents and teachers as well. Behavior therapy has been proven to be effective. You will learn more about this in the next chapter.

PHARMACOLOGICAL TREATMENTS

There are several pharmacological treatments available for children with ADHD. Each treatment carries various positive and possible side effects. They have all been tested and proven to be effective in treating ADHD symptoms. When taking these medications, regular doctor visits should be scheduled until the symptoms have improved. From then on, visits should take place every three to six months. It is important to call your child's doctor immediately if you have any concerns or questions, are contemplating any changes in your child's treatment, or notice any side effects.

Stimulants

Stimulants are the most commonly recommended type of medication for ADHD. There are limited side effects, and results can be seen quickly. Stimulants help balance and boost the chemicals in your child's brain and typically target symptoms of hyperactivity and lack of attention and focus. Research has shown that stimulants relieve the symptoms in 70–80% of children with ADHD. Short-acting stimulants provide a release that lasts up to four hours. After the four hours have passed, your child may need to take another dose. Sustained-release stimulants can be taken once in the morning. The two types of stimulant medications are methylphenidates and amphetamines. Both are found to work in the same way. However, a person might react better to one than the other.

▷ **Methylphenidate**

Methylphenidate stimulates the central nervous system. It provides more dopamine and norepinephrine to the brain in doses that mimic those produced by a neurotypical brain. This stimulates those parts of the ADHD brain that are not as active as those of the neurotypical brain. Your child is better able to concentrate and less impulsive. Because methylphenidate prevents chemicals from being absorbed too quickly back into the nerve cells, it helps the brain to communicate effectively. This, in turn, can positively affect your child's heart, lungs, and stomach, though it can also have a few side effects. Some examples of methylphenidate medicine are Focalin, Ritalin, and Concerta.

▷ **Amphetamines**

Like methylphenidate, amphetamines also stimulate the central nervous system by aiding in the release of dopamine and norepinephrine. They can help promote nerve growth and brain development and prevent undesired changes in the structure and function of your child's brain. Some examples of amphetamine medications are Adderall XR, Mydayis, and Dexedrine.

▷ **Health Risks of Stimulant Medications**

Stimulant medications can affect those with underlying heart conditions as they can increase heart rate and blood pressure. They can also affect those with psychiatric problems by increasing manic episodes or causing agitation. Stimulant medications may also negatively affect people with glaucoma or Tourette's syndrome. Side effects of stimulants include headaches, loss of appetite and weight loss, nervousness, tics, and sleep problems. Most of these side effects can be relieved by changing the dosage and the time the medication is taken, or by switching to another stimulant. Stimulants may also delay your child's growth and cause allergic reactions. In the case of their growth, your child will eventually attain their natural height, just at a slightly slower pace.

Non-Stimulant Medications

Non-stimulant medications include antidepressants like bupropion (Wellbutrin XL and SR), clonidine (Kapvay, Catapres), atomoxetine (Strattera), and guanfacine (Intuniv). These are slower-acting than stimulants, and it may take several weeks before you see a definite change in your child's symptoms. These are typically recommended after stimulants have been tried. Non-stimulant medications can be used if your child has health problems or has experienced side effects that prevent them from taking stimulants.

Non-Stimulant Risk

Research has not proven this to be the case, but there are concerns about an increase in suicidal thoughts for children on non-stimulant medications. If your child shows any signs of depression or thoughts of suicide, contact your healthcare provider immediately.

The Safe Use of Medications

Stimulant medications are controlled substances. Your child can safely take these without the risk of abuse and addiction as long as the doctor's recommendations are followed. Regular checkups also help ensure that the medication is being used safely, and the doctor can assess if any changes in dosage and stimulant type are necessary. As a parent, you should make sure you are in charge of and supervise your child taking their medication. The medications should be kept out of reach and stored in a secure location. If the school needs a supply of your child's medication, you should bring it there yourself instead of sending it with your child. Only give the medication as the doctor has prescribed it. If you believe any changes are necessary, contact your doctor before doing anything else. Do not try to double or catch up on doses. If a dosage has been missed, ensure your child takes only the prescribed amount when they do get the medication.

If you are starting a new stimulant, you can schedule it at a time when your child does not have school or any planned activities. This allows you to observe how the child responds. If you believe your child needs a break from taking the medication, you can also do this when the child has no activities or school. You should also try as best as possible to create and keep a strict medication schedule.

The Monarch eTNS System

The Monarch external Trigeminal Nerve Stimulation System is a new device available via prescription only. It is the size of a cell phone and is prescribed to children 7–12 years old who are not on ADHD prescription medicine. This device is used by parents when the child is asleep. A small patch on the child's forehead sends low-level electrical stimulation which sends signals through the child's brain. This is intended to help the child's behavior, emotion, and attention levels. If you are considering using the eTNS system, consult your healthcare provider to learn more about its uses and possible side effects (Mayo Clinic Staff, n.d.).

NON-PHARMACOLOGICAL TREATMENTS

Non-pharmacological treatments can be used alongside medications for ADHD. In fact, these treatments are recommended before medication for children under six years old. Deciding whether to use non-pharmacological treatments with or without medication is a decision you can make after consulting with your healthcare provider. These treatments serve to give your child agency in controlling their actions. It provides you, your child, and those around them with tools to help your child live a successful life. Non-pharmacological treatments provide intervention for the educational, behavioral, social, lifestyle, and psychological needs of your child and your family. Treatments can be modified as your child ages.

Behavioral Therapy

▷ **Parent-Led Behavioral Interventions**

In this practice, parents are taught behavior management techniques to help their children. The training is led by a therapist and occurs in eight or more sessions. It can be done individually or in groups with other families. Your therapist will teach you how to use structure, positive reinforcement, and consistency to help your child and give techniques for positive interaction with them. A good therapist communicates regularly with the family and provides activities for you to practice with your child. This intervention is especially important for younger children who are not mature enough to manage their behaviors without a parent's help. It targets the core ADHD symptoms along with defiant behavior.

▷ **Classroom-Led Behavioral Interventions**

While the classroom is a controlled environment, the teacher has several students and a curriculum that sets out a list of goals that the teacher is expected to meet yearly. Children are engaged in many activities, including playtime and field trips. This environment is different from the one at home and can cause your child to react in a way that they may not at home. It can also be challenging for a teacher who has to divide their attention among several students. Classroom-led behavioral intervention can provide support for the school, the teacher, your child, and the other students. It provides a context and helps teach your child how to behave and respond in different situations. The situations presented are real-life scenarios. The aim is to equip your child with the skills necessary to navigate the outside world. Your child is taught how to manage social interactions, follow rules, organize themselves, engage in and complete activities, and other areas necessary for general life. Teachers trained in these interventions can lead them at the school.

▷ **Cognitive Behavioral Therapy (CBT)**

With cognitive behavioral therapy, your child is taught how to evaluate their thoughts. They learn to identify which thoughts cause negative feelings and how to deal with them by thinking more positively. A child is given behavioral tools to self-regulate and cope with diverse situations and environments. These tools can help ease their anxiety and redirect their focus.

▷ **Neurofeedback**

With neurofeedback, your child's brain activity is monitored while they perform various tasks. Sensors on the scalp tell your healthcare provider when your child's brain waves are performing at an optimal level. Your child is then taught to recognize and practice the behaviors that cause their brain to perform at that level. Neurofeedback helps your child train their brain to complete tasks, focus, control impulses, and perform executive functions effectively.

▷ **Psychoeducation**

Psychoeducation is providing ADHD information to your child and your family. This information can be given in the form of internet sources, books, videos, and other print, visual, and auditory media. This helps clear up misconceptions and provides reliable, helpful information about ADHD to you and your family. Knowledge is power, and by educating your family, your healthcare provider is enabling you and your child to make informed decisions. Psychoeducation includes you, your child, your family, and others with regular contact with your child. The information given is tailored to the age and maturity level of your child and addresses different situations and environments. The sharing of information comes directly from a healthcare provider and can be done in group sessions (ADHD Institute, n.d.).

Exercise and Diet

▷ **Nutrition and Dietary Interventions**

While more research is needed in this area, it's recommended that you practice good nutrition and ensure your child has a balanced diet. Your child's meals should be rich in grains, fruits, vegetables, omega-3, and other healthy fatty acids. You should try to limit the intake of processed food and sugars.

Initial research proposes that ADHD symptoms can be linked to deficiencies in magnesium, zinc, vitamin B6, and iron. Therefore, ensuring your child has a healthy intake of food containing these nutrients might reduce symptoms. Drinking an adequate amount of water is also recommended as the brain's functions slow when dehydrated. Omega-3 fatty acids are found in eggs, flaxseed, salmon, sardines, and other foods. These are shown to improve brain function and can help manage your child's concentration, hyperactivity, and impulsiveness. Complex carbohydrates and proteins decrease hyperactivity and increase alertness. You can maintain your child's blood sugar levels by scheduling meals three hours apart. Your child may have food allergies which can negatively affect their symptoms. Allergens should be identified and eliminated from their diet. You should talk to your healthcare provider when planning or considering any changes to your child's diet.

▷ **Exercise**

Engaging in physical activities can help with memory, concentration, mood, planning, and time management. It can limit impulsiveness, hyperactivity, anxiety, and depression. Exercise helps boost and balance blood flow along with the dopamine and norepinephrine chemicals in your child's brain.

If your child is not getting enough exercise at school, you can schedule physical activities outside of school. While you could go to the gym or hire a personal trainer, you can also have your child exercise at home. Your child should get at least one hour of exercise daily. Vary your child's exercises to prevent them from getting bored, and stick to an exercise plan. You can begin by exercising for a few minutes at a time, then encourage your child to exercise more until your child has reached a set goal. The exercises you set for your child can incorporate sports, games, and dancing to make it more enjoyable. You can also keep their attention by splitting the exercises into 15-minute intervals.

Additional Non-Medicated Treatments

Sleep is a very important factor that affects how your brain functions. You can teach your child good sleeping habits by keeping the bedroom cool and dark, having a consistent bedtime schedule, and creating a ritual or bedtime routine that helps your child to relax and unwind. Avoid screen time directly before bed and remove distracting technological devices from their bedroom. A good night's rest can lower your child's symptoms of impulsiveness and restlessness. Practicing meditation and mindfulness can also help increase your child's focus and maintain self-awareness and self-regulation.

SUMMARY

Deciding on the best treatments for your child can be difficult. You may struggle with feelings of guilt and inadequacy. In those moments, it is important to focus on your child and evaluate if the methods you have chosen are working. You can choose medical and non-medical options in treating your child. Stimulant medications are prescribed medications that work quickly to boost and balance your child's brain chemicals. This lessens the symptoms of ADHD your child is experiencing. There are side effects to stimulants, which can be dealt with by talking to your healthcare provider. ADHD medication is not a one-size-fits-all solution. Each person reacts differently and requires different doses. It's important to ask your child how the medication is working, observe them closely, and contact your healthcare professional if you're considering any changes to the stimulant your child is taking. Non-stimulant medications like antidepressants take a longer time to work. They are typically prescribed if your child has challenges with taking stimulants.

Whatever the medication, you should take steps to ensure that your child is taking them safely. You should administer doses yourself or supervise your child whenever they are taking medication. Stick to the schedule and the dosage and personally bring any medication the school needs. Keep the medicine in a secure location, and do not try to overcompensate if a dosage has been missed.

There are also several other treatments for your child. These include intervention programs where parents are taught how to manage and communicate positively with their children. Trained teachers can also provide support and programs at your child's school. Neurofeedback and cognitive behavioral therapy can teach your child to monitor their own behavior and thoughts to reduce negative thoughts and think more positively. There is also an eTNS device that can stimulate your child's brain while they sleep. Psychoeducation provides you, your child, your family, your child's teachers, and others with information that helps you make informed decisions.

Making changes to your child's diet can help lessen their symptoms. You should ensure their meals are balanced and scheduled. Proper daily exercise is also recommended. Keeping a regular sleep schedule, practicing bedtime rituals, and engaging in mindfulness and meditation can also help with symptoms of ADHD.

There are many treatment options available for you and your child. The next chapter focuses on one non-pharmacological treatment: behavioral therapy.

5

BEHAVIORAL THERAPY

Because my daughter was six when she was diagnosed, our doctor recommended behavioral therapy. At first, I was skeptical. Can ADHD really be managed by teaching the power of positive thinking? I decided to see what it was all about and realized my view of behavioral therapy was too simplistic. It was much more comprehensive than I thought, and even better—it worked!

The decision of how your child's ADHD should be treated ultimately lies with you. Not everyone is comfortable with using medication. After all, there are side effects to consider. As mentioned in the previous chapter, your child may experience trouble sleeping, headaches, upset stomach, weight loss, irritability, dry mouth, and nervousness. There are even the more serious, though rare, side effects of seizures, suicidal thoughts, hallucinations, allergic reactions, and increased blood pressure.

These are very concerning effects to consider. However, as mentioned, they can be addressed by talking to your doctor about adjusting the dosage or changing the medication. Medications are still an important part of treating ADHD, and each reaction is different. As such, doctors address any issues on a case-by-case basis.

I allowed my daughter to begin taking stimulants when she was twelve. At first, I was worried when she complained of headaches and lost her appetite. I felt as though I had failed her, like I had drugged my daughter and now she was experiencing negative effects. After all, behavior therapy had been working. She was learning how to self-regulate and think positively. After talking to our healthcare provider, I agreed to keep her on medication but adjust the dosage. It took some trial and error, but eventually, we discovered what worked for her. The improvement was almost immediate. Where she had been doing well, she was now doing great. I came to realize that a combination of behavioral therapy and stimulants was what was best for her. She was happier and felt more in control of herself. Even her teachers remarked on the difference.

WHAT IS BEHAVIORAL THERAPY?

You may have heard that behaviors are learned. Behavioral therapy operates on this idea; it's a therapy used to treat various mental disorders by helping individuals to self-evaluate themselves, identify negative thoughts, and promote positive thinking. This allows them to change undesirable behaviors. Behavioral therapy is used to treat panic and anger-related disorders, anxiety, and depression. It can also treat phobias, self-harming behaviors, and disorders relating to eating, post-traumatic stress, obsessive compulsions, substance abuse, bipolar, and ADHD.

TYPES OF BEHAVIORAL THERAPY

Cognitive Behavioral Therapy (CBT)

This type of therapy focuses on patterns of thought and action. Your actions and moods are influenced by your thoughts and beliefs. Therefore, it is possible to manage your thinking and create new patterns of thoughts and habits. Cognitive behavioral therapy teaches your child to think about immediate problems and work out solutions. Doing so will improve your child's quality of life.

Cognitive Behavioral Play Therapy

For this type of behavioral therapy, your child is asked to play while being observed by their therapist. This observation helps the therapist identify areas of comfort and discomfort for your child. They can learn what your child has difficulty expressing.

Your child is free to choose their toys and method of play. They are also asked to draw or use the sandbox to create images. Your therapist will then teach you how to communicate with your child through games and teach you and your child coping skills and strategies for meeting goals.

Acceptance and Commitment Therapy (ACT)

Acceptance and commitment therapy builds on cognitive theory by not only asking your child to identify negative thoughts but to accept these thoughts. Your child is asked to focus on their values and use these values to help them through life. Practicing mindfulness and acknowledging negative thoughts will help your child gain control until the negativity in their minds no longer has power over them. Accepting their ADHD is a big part of ACT. Your child is also asked to commit to achieving certain goals and taking certain actions.

Dialectical Behavioral

This therapy was initi[ally...]
borderline personalit[y...]
in treating other di[sorders...]
child is taught copi[ng...]
emotions, examining [...]
mindfulness, and [...]
communications an[d...]
2022).

Systematic Desensiti[zation]

Certain triggers [...]
react negati[vely...]
your chil[d...]
sensiti[ve...]
re[...]

BEHAVIORAL THERAPY TECHNIQUES

Aversion Therapy

With this technique, your child is taught to create negative associations for behaviors or thoughts that might make them feel good but are unhealthy or undesirable. For example, your child might feel good after throwing a tantrum. The therapist will encourage them to associate these tantrums with something that they hate doing. As a result, whenever your child thinks about throwing a tantrum, they will immediately remember something negative that will stop them from going through with it.

...and stimuli can cause your child to ...vely. Systematic desensitization teaches ...d to become more accustomed to and less ...ve to these stimuli. Your child will be taught ...axation and breathing techniques that will help them change their negative responses to more relaxed, positive ones. Eventually, your child will slowly confront and master their fears and triggers under the guidance of their therapist.

EFFECTIVENESS OF BEHAVIORAL THERAPY

Behavioral therapy has been thoroughly researched and is considered highly effective. It is used to treat a variety of mental conditions. Play therapy is very effective for children aged 3–12 years old and is increasingly being recommended. Research has shown that 75% of people see improvement after engaging in cognitive behavioral therapy.

Behavioral therapy is effective in treating anxiety, depression, substance abuse, bulimia, disorders relating to anger, and stress. It's also effective in helping those who experience physical symptoms due to their thoughts.

CHILDREN AND BEHAVIORAL THERAPY

Play and applied behavioral therapy are commonly used for children. Your child is taught how to respond positively to many different situations and environments. They learn how to adapt to stimuli while letting go of behaviors that prevent them from adjusting to different environments. This therapy involves more than the child. You, your family, your child's teachers, and other adults closely associated with the child are asked to participate. Your therapist will work diligently to ensure that the child trusts them enough to open up to them so they can help.

FINDING A BEHAVIORAL THERAPIST

You can ask your primary healthcare provider if you are unsure how to go about finding a therapist. They will recommend someone appropriate. There is an online tool, The Healthline FindCare tool, that can help. You can also approach faith- or non-faith-based counselors, social workers, psychologists, and psychiatrists. A psychiatrist can write prescriptions if they believe one is necessary. Ensure that whoever you choose has the appropriate training and background matching your needs.

In creating an individualized plan for your child and your family, your therapist will ask detailed questions. It's okay to try several therapists until you find one you're comfortable with and until you and your child are seeing improvements.

Mental health is covered under most insurance plans, and some therapists offer payment options and grants to families in need (Gotter & Burford, 2022).

BEHAVIORAL PARENT TRAINING FOR ADHD

As a parent, your role in your child's well-being and learned behavior is extremely important. Your words and actions shape their thoughts and influence their future. As a parent of a child with ADHD, your role becomes much more vital. They need extra guidance in self-regulating their emotions and in knowing what action is appropriate in different contexts. They need someone to love them and to let them know they are not simply bad. Your child needs role models. They may attend programs and learn strategies, but it is you, the parent, who helps them practice what they have learned and provides feedback on what they're doing well and what needs improvement. A child can achieve success despite their parents, but it's so much more powerful when that success is achieved with the help of their parents.

By researching and going to training, you learn how to communicate with your child, understand them, help them manage their behaviors, and help them communicate positively with others. This is where Behavioral Parent Training (BPT) comes in. It is usually done in groups facilitated by a professional who may hold the sessions in person or online.

BPT teaches you how to set up effective house rules and a system of rewards for when those rules are followed. You learn to focus on your child's positive behaviors and improvements rather than on their negative ones. You learn lifelong skills such as working alongside your child's teacher to create daily behavioral report cards. BPT teaches you how to create daily routines; give clear, specific instructions; and create rewards and disciplinary actions that are age-appropriate. You will also learn how to minimize distractions and create an organized home, limit choices to prevent your child from being overwhelmed, and encourage positive behaviors through acknowledgment and reward. BPT also teaches you how to break down large tasks into smaller ones that your child can more easily manage. Behavioral Parent Training seeks to help the child by training you, the parent.

How Behavioral Parent Training Works

In BPT, the meetings are held once a week for 8–12 weeks by a professional who trains a group of 15–30 parents. Each session addresses one skill. The professional uses videos to show a parent interacting with their child and making common mistakes. You are asked to comment on what happened in the video, what the parent did right and what they did wrong, and what you would do if you were in that situation. The professional then shares strategies on the skill being looked at and allows you to practice through brainstorming, role play, or other ways. Each parent is then asked to go home and use what they have learned for that session. The next meeting begins with you all discussing your use of the strategy, its effectiveness, and what you could do differently in the future.

This group session and practice allows the parents to bond and share their experiences and tips. You can support each other as well as get support from the professional. Parents no longer feel alone and are encouraged by each other.

The daily report card is an important part of this training. This card is created by both you and the teacher. You will identify desirable behaviors you want the child to develop. This includes how they interact and build relationships with adults. You may want your child to be polite, follow instructions, and obey class rules. You may also want to see improvement in how your child interacts with their peers. This improvement could include being kind and waiting for turns during recess, speaking politely with other children, and not interrupting when someone else is talking. Another area in which you might want to see improvement is your child's academic work. This could include completing classwork and assignments or having all the necessary supplies.

The reward system for the daily report card is carried out by both you and the teacher. The teacher makes notes on the card as to whether or not your child has met their daily goals. This note can be a simple sentence, a happy or sad face, a checkmark, or other marks and words. Whenever your child has achieved the goals for the day, you would reward them at home, too. This reward is whatever you deem appropriate. It could be more TV time, a favorite snack, a game, or something else.

The Expected Results of BPT

The effectiveness of BPT is dependent on how severe your child's symptoms are, the consistency of rules and rewards between home and school, your commitment to the program, and other factors. Sometimes medication and different forms of behavioral therapy are necessary to help your child. Research shows that children who receive behavioral therapy before medication actually need lower doses of stimulants or non-stimulants.

You should not expect miracles to happen instantly after starting behavioral parent therapy. Teaching and learning take practice, and you will see improvement over time. Your child may display an "extinction burst" where their behavior gets worse before it gets better. Because you're learning to ignore negative behavior and focus on the positive, your child might act out just to get your attention. These difficult periods do not last very long, and you can get through them by keeping to the strategies you have been taught. Once your child realizes that they gain attention through positive behaviors, they will try to practice these behaviors more frequently. As a result, you and your child will have healthier, happier communications.

It's very important that you remain patient and do not allow yourself to become discouraged when you think there is no progress or when your child appears to be regressing. Start small and take it one step at a time. Focus on the little changes and celebrate small wins. There is a reason why the saying "Rome wasn't built in a day" is so popular. The techniques learned in BPT can help you improve as a parent. You can make informed decisions in guiding your child through childhood and into the universally challenging teenhood.

Which Goes First: Medication or BPT?

The Centers for Disease Control (CDC) found that 75% of children with ADHD are treated with medication only. As mentioned in the previous chapter, the American Psychiatrist Association recommends behavior therapy as the first treatment for children under six and a combination of medication and behavior therapy for children over six. While either on their own can be helpful, remarkable results can be seen when both are used together.

Research recommends trying behavioral parent training first. If medication is tried and fails, treating ADHD becomes much harder. It has been shown that if a parent sees improvement with the medication, they may be less committed to the training, especially when the medication is showing faster results. This makes having behavioral parent training after medication less effective. It was also seen that raising the dosage of the medication does not improve the child's behavior. As a result, many healthcare professionals recommend starting behavioral parent training first.

Finding the BPT Program That's the Right Fit for You

You can call a local teaching hospital or ask your pediatrician for a recommendation for a BPT program. Talk to the professional conducting the training and look for the keyword 'behavioral' during the conversation. Ensure that what they are teaching is evidence-based. This means the techniques they are teaching have been proven effective for treating children with ADHD through extensive scientific research by professionals. You should also decide whether you want to participate in individual or group training sessions. As behavioral therapy is most effective if started before your child is six, consider your child's age when starting the program. Discover the cost of the training and consider how it matches your schedule.

This book is a comprehensive, extensively researched resource aimed at helping you raise a superstar child with ADHD. Attending behavioral parent training is an additional resource that will greatly help your child (Flynn, 2022).

SUMMARY

Behavioral therapy relies on the idea that behavior is learned and can therefore be changed. Your child is taught to face their fears, acknowledge their negative thoughts, and turn them into positive ones. This therapy is recommended to be used before medication, especially for children under six. There are several types of behavioral therapy. Cognitive behavioral therapy teaches your child to form positive patterns of thought and behavior and to work out solutions to immediate problems. Cognitive behavioral play therapy involves your child playing with toys, drawing, and similar activities while being observed by a therapist who will note how your child expresses themselves during play. Acceptance and commitment therapy asks your child to focus on their values, use these values to help guide them through life, and make commitments to achieving goals. Dialectical behavioral therapy helps your child to cope with different situations by regulating their emotions, practicing mindfulness, working on their interpersonal relationships, and learning the limits of their distress tolerance.

Behavioral therapy uses aversion therapy to help your child create negative associations for pleasurable but unhealthy behaviors. It also uses systematic desensitization to make your child less sensitive to stimuli that will typically trigger a negative response.

Research has shown that 75% of people who have engaged in behavioral therapy have seen improvements. Play therapy is especially effective for children.

Behavioral therapy is also used to treat anger-related disorders, anxiety, stress, depression, and other mental illnesses.

With behavioral therapy, your child is taught how to cope and respond to many different situations and environments. They learn life skills that help them throughout their lives. Finding a therapist who is right for you is very important. You can consult your healthcare provider, use online tools, or reach out to social workers, faith- and non-faith-based counselors, psychologists, and psychiatrists. It's okay to try several therapists until you find one that is right for you and your family.

Behavioral parent training operates on the thought that by training the parent, you are helping the child. This is led by a trained professional and can be done individually or in groups. The sessions last 8–12 weeks and are typically done with groups of 15–30 parents. One skill is addressed each week. The parents watch a video modeling interactions between a parent and child. They are asked to comment on the video, then are provided strategies by the professional. After modeling these strategies, parents are asked to go home, practice what they have learned, then return and discuss the results.

BPT has been proven to be very effective in helping you and your child. You should, however, be patient as the results may not be immediate, and your child's behavior may get worse before it gets better. In finding the BPT program that is right for you, you may talk to your pediatrician. You can also talk to the person conducting the program, find out if their strategies are evidence-based, and consider the age of your child before starting the training. The cost and whether the sessions fit your schedule should also be considered.

Behavioral therapy and medication have been proven to be very effective when used together. The choice of how your child receives treatment is in your hands. You can begin helping your child by teaching them how to manage their intense emotions. You will learn more about how to do this in the next chapter.

6

MANAGING INTENSE EMOTIONS

With my daughter constantly switching elementary schools because she was "not the right fit," I became worried about how her education was being affected. I decided to put aside a special time in the evenings to work on her reading and basic math. It was a struggle getting her to pay attention, but through research and trial and error, I discovered strategies that she enjoyed. My daughter began devouring everything I showed her, especially anything having to do with reading. I felt so proud of myself. But then, the meltdown happened. After a week of focusing solely on reading, I took her book away and told her we would be doing math. For me, it seemed like such a simple thing. We were just switching to something else that she needed to learn, and she had been doing so well. I was surprised when she flung the book across the room, threw herself down, and began to cry at the top of her lungs.

At first, I was frozen. My daughter had had meltdowns before, of course. She could not always handle her emotions. Sometimes the tantrums occurred in public, and I would be thoroughly embarrassed. The judgment in people's eyes always got to me. Worse was when someone tried to step in and calm her. It was as if they believed I was a terrible mother and they could do a better job. Sometimes she ignored them, but at other times my darling traitor of a daughter would calm down and flash them puppy dog eyes. They would then get this smirk and look at me with contempt. In those moments, I would grit my teeth, smile, say thank you, and get out of there as fast as I could.

Somehow I was prepared for the public meltdowns, but I was unprepared for her reaction to a change in her studies. I felt stirrings of anger. It was just a simple change; we would get back to reading later. However, I knew if I expressed my anger, she would shut down completely, and we wouldn't get anything done. I took deep breaths and tried to see things from her point of view: She had been enjoying herself, and the fact that she was able to understand what was being taught gave her confidence. So many things were difficult for her, and it made her doubt her intelligence. This was proof that she could learn, just like everyone else. What was a simple switch for me was the loss of something important for her.

So rather than responding sharply, I asked her to choose a pillow and sat back as she vented her frustration. Once she was finished, we talked. I told her I understood and let her know how proud I was of her. I informed her of the importance of math, and how it could help her in her daily life, at school, and in the future. Then I promised a fun activity once we were finished. I used a game on her device to draw her interest and promised her we would get back to working on reading next week. She calmed down, apologized, and engaged happily in the lesson. I let out a deep breath. Crisis contained. From then on, I made sure to pause and carefully explain any changes in our studies to her. I worked with her on taking deep breaths and saying the word 'calm' to herself. This helped her accept the changes, and eventually, I no longer needed to stop and explain.

The sensations your child experiences are more intense, and they react accordingly. This just means that they need some extra steps to help them to process what they're feeling. It can be challenging for you but helping your child manage their emotions and reactions can be done. By understanding how the brain regulates emotions, you can learn why your child reacts the way they do and help your child learn how to handle their feelings.

EMOTIONS AND ADHD

Emotional Dysregulation

People with ADHD have difficulty interpreting their feelings and may react to things inappropriately. The inability to control one's emotions is known as "emotional dysregulation," and it is closely related to ADHD. 70% of adults with ADHD experience emotional dysregulation, and children also experience dysregulation due to ADHD symptoms. For a child with ADHD, this can lead to meltdowns, as they are unable to pause, process what they're feeling, and come up with an appropriate response. Having public meltdowns can make this dysregulation even worse. Your child's feelings are not wrong; they are simply intense. However, their expression of this feeling can result in them feeling guilty and ashamed afterward (Ditzel, 2022).

You can identify your child's emotional dysregulation by observing their patterns of behavior. This is most clearly seen in your child's impulsiveness. Other signs include persistence of negative emotions, trouble regaining emotional balance, heavy focus on conflicts, and limited resilience.

Other Emotional Effects and Reactions

Your child may also find it difficult to calm themselves when they're angry or annoyed. Getting motivated when bored is challenging, as is reining in strong emotions. They will spend a lot of time focusing on seemingly small issues and get easily frustrated over things that appear insignificant. Gentle criticism may cause offense and upset, and your child will feel a strong urge to immediately receive something they want. These things may result in your child feeling anxious, depressed, angry, or remorseful. They are aware of what is happening to them but are unable to control it. It's easy for your child to get overwhelmed and give up when facing difficulty, and they may avoid socializing with others. Not only are the emotions your child experiences more intense, but they last longer, leading to disruption in their daily life.

Why Emotions Are Challenging for A Child With ADHD

Your child's brain develops differently from the neurotypical brain. This affects how their brain carries out executive functions. As a result, your child is more prone to giving in to impulses and taking risks. They have trouble stepping back and viewing things from a different perspective. Instead, they give in to their immediate reactions. Your child's working memory is also affected. Your child's immediate focus is in the moment, and they do not take the time to consider their other emotions or the long-term effects.

The strongest immediate reaction your child feels towards a situation floods their brain, blocking out all other emotions and reason. This causes your child to give in to the emotion and ignore any thoughts that caution them to consider their reactions. Your child may be less tolerant, hot-tempered, and more prone to frustration. The communication regarding emotions in their brain is more limited, which may cause them to seem unaware of how others are feeling. Your child is extremely sensitive to anything they perceive to be criticism and will react defensively. Shifting their focus from one emotion to another is difficult for them, and they may react without listening to explanations. Appearing to be incompetent or foolish by others is also a fear your child carries. They are aware of the strength of their emotions and the challenges they have regulating them and will avoid these emotions. This results in them having difficulties with any situations that they find to be stressful.

Distinguishing between high- and low-level threats is also difficult, causing your child to always be on high alert. As a result, your child has trouble acting rationally in stressful situations. Your child may be frustrated with themselves, leading to low self-esteem, anxiety, and depression. They may only engage in activities that provide them with instant rewards and gratification. Otherwise, they have trouble mustering the motivation to begin and complete tasks. Their motivation is also affected by the lower levels of dopamine in their brains. Their working memory is not developed enough to help them with organization, focus, and self-regulation. As a result, they will lose their temper and be disorganized (Brown, 2022).

TEACHING YOUR CHILD EMOTIONAL REGULATION SKILLS

The ability to process your emotions and adapt to situations and environments is known as "self-regulation." Having self-regulation means being able to handle frustrations, accept changes, accept when expectations are not met, resist having outbursts when confronted with negative stimuli, and calm yourself when upset and angry. In the neurotypical brain, this skill is acquired as a child grows, and they're able to direct their emotions.

Your ability to self-regulate is affected by your personality and the environment in which you are raised. Some children have trouble calming themselves, and this can follow them through life. Some are raised by parents who give in easily to tantrums or over-soothe their children. This, in turn, affects the child's ability to learn and practice self-discipline.

Due to how their brain works, children with ADHD may have difficulty practicing self-regulation.

Self-regulation can be taught in much the same way as any other skill. You can help your child control their emotions by teaching them to pause, consider their thoughts and the situation, and choose an appropriate response. Rather than avoiding difficult situations, teach your child to accept and address these situations. Help them to work through them. As your child gains confidence and improves with self-regulating, pull back your support and allow them to stand on their own. This technique is called 'scaffolding.' Scaffolding involves providing your child with strategies and helping them to use these strategies in the initial stages. Knowing when to step back is an important part of this technique.

Allowing your child to practice what you taught them helps them to be more efficient in self-regulating and more independent. You can do this by introducing them to stimuli they consider to be negative in a controlled environment. You can take your child on outings intended for them to practice the skills you've taught them. Points can be awarded for each goal they accomplish. If your child is having difficulties completing a task, you can break the task down into smaller parts and walk your child through each part. Eventually, you can have them practice the task as a whole.

By being patient and calm, you can help your child learn to be more adaptive. By providing them positive feedback and gently listing areas of improvement, you can teach your child to be more self-reflective. Your child will better be able to slow down and think about their emotions and how to respond to stimuli.

You can help your child develop emotional intelligence by teaching them how to examine and attach an accurate label to what they're feeling. You can help them build their emotional vocabulary and create a home environment that is accepting of all types of emotions. Let your child know that it's okay to have both positive and negative feelings. Model emotional control for them to understand. The therapies discussed in the previous chapter can also help your child learn to regulate their emotions. Medication and practicing mindfulness are also tools that can help your child process and manage their feelings.

You should show your child that their feelings are valid. It's important that you allow them to express themselves and then try to see things from their point of view. There are many coping skills you can teach your child that will help them in stressful situations. These include music, deep breathing, exercise, drawing, talking to you or a peer, and journaling. It's also important to take care of your own emotional health, as this will affect and influence your child.

THREE PROSOCIAL EMOTIONS FOR EMOTIONAL REGULATION

Gratitude

Being thankful can keep you from feeling empty and constantly searching for what you do not have. You can teach your child gratitude by writing down the things you both are grateful for on pieces of paper and putting them in a gratitude jar. You can encourage your child to give thanks for something daily and write daily thank-you notes. Teaching your child to write notes acknowledging acts of kindness can help them develop gratitude. Your child can also create an art piece of all the people who support them and hang it up somewhere in the house. As a family, you can have a board where one member writes something they need help with, and another member can sign their name as an indication that they are willing to help. This can serve as a visual reminder of the support the family provides for each other.

As humans, our survival instincts are strong. We are constantly on the lookout for danger, which can lead to a lot of negative thoughts crowding the brain. Being grateful helps you and your child focus on the positives in life and can make you happier and more peaceful. Gratitude has been shown to reduce stress, anxiety, pain, and depression. It helps you focus on positive memories and improves your mental and physical health. Dopamine and serotonin are released from your brain when you experience gratitude, making you feel happier and more focused, and can help form good habits. By practicing gratitude, you encourage your brain to push these positive brain chemicals through your system. This results in an improvement in your brain structure and your ability to regulate your emotions and perform executive functions.

Gratitude and the ADHD Brain

The increase in dopamine caused by practicing gratitude helps the development of your child's prefrontal cortex. It helps your child to focus less on being afraid of rejection and more on positive things. This positivity will help your child to be more focused and productive when tackling tasks and activities. It will also help them be less anxious and more resilient. Practicing gratitude helps keep your child's mind off their failures and helps them feel more balanced and accepting of themselves.

Having ADHD makes it more difficult to focus on feeling gratitude. Working with your child on daily gratitude practices will help them incorporate gratitude into their general mindset and outlook on life.

Pride

Teaching your child to have pride in themselves will help build their self-esteem. Too often, children with ADHD believe there is something wrong with them, which can lead to anxiety, depression, anger, and emotional outbursts. You can teach your child to develop pride by allowing them to showcase their skills and share their knowledge of something that interests them. Let them feel like they are the expert. You can also give your child important tasks to carry out. They will feel mature and independent and gain confidence in themselves because you have shown that you trust them. This also gives them a chance to work on their life skills. You can also make a skills board and highlight all the things they've accomplished.

You can build your child's self-confidence and pride by praising them when they have put effort into doing things. You can encourage their strengths by focusing on the things they are good at. Praising them to other people will also build their confidence. Teach them to learn from their mistakes by viewing their failures as lessons that will guide them. Accepting your child for who they are also helps them accept themselves. You can move slowly when introducing them to new things and use scaffolding to guide them. Having reasonable expectations will also help your child. You can engage your child in activities that help them interact and build relationships with others. This includes activities that require them to help other people. When your child reaches out to you, give them your full attention so they know what they have to say is valid.

Compassion

Empathy is one of your child's superpowers and helping them develop this will improve their self-control and their interactions with others. By presenting your family unit as a team and doing activities together, you can teach your child the value of compassion and support. Games that start conversations can also help your child learn more about others and develop methods of communication. You can try a game of Truth or Dare or Never Have I Ever. Teach your child how to show compassion towards themselves by accepting their mistakes, strengths, and challenges. Engage them in conversations about the strengths and weaknesses of others; this will help them to understand themselves and the people around them. Mindful meditation will also help your child feel more attuned to their environment and the people in it.

Empathy and ADHD

Empathy is the ability to put yourself in someone else's shoes and see and feel things the way they do. On the other end of the spectrum is narcissism. A narcissistic person is so concentrated on themselves that they are unable to consider the emotions of others.

The symptoms of ADHD can result in children showing a lack of empathy. While some children with ADHD can display narcissistic tendencies, this is not always the case. Hyperactivity, impulsiveness, short attention spans, and emotional outbursts can appear to be signs of narcissism. The connection between empathy and ADHD is a challenging one, and this can result in problems with relationships and communication. Your child may have difficulty connecting with friends and family members and maintaining relationships.

Fortunately, there are things you can do that will help your child practice compassion and empathy. You can model empathy by showing attention, appreciation, and care for your child. Express thanks for the things each family member does. Rather than accusing the child when they've done something wrong, acknowledge that they have made a mistake and work out solutions going forward. Use a tone that is firm but caring when giving corrections. Allow your child to see you helping other people. While you're doing so, provide opportunities for your child to also help others and give back to the people around them. Join in on volunteer opportunities. If you're worried about how your child might react to certain situations while helping out, try to find activities that you feel are ones they would be able to handle and feel comfortable in. Take special care to acknowledge and praise your child as this will help them feel good about themselves. Talking about feelings and celebrating each other's achievements will also help them build empathy. By working with your child, being patient, and seeking help for their symptoms, you can turn your child's ADHD and empathy into a superpower (Buzanko, 2021).

THE FRUSTRATION LOG

Identifying your child's patterns of behavior and what triggers them will help you teach them how to manage their intense emotions. The following Frustration Log will help you track your child's behavior and understand why they are frustrated.

When	Setting	What Did Your Child Do?	Strategies/ Response
• Time • Day • Month & Year	• Where was your child? • What were they doing before the outburst? • Who was with them?	• How did your child verbally and/or physically express their frustrations?	• How did you respond to your child's display? • How was your child able to calm down? • What strategies did you use, and how effective were they? • How will you address a similar situation in the future?

MINDFULNESS EXERCISES FOR CHILDREN WITH ADHD

As mentioned before, mindfulness is a great way to help your child manage their ADHD symptoms and build compassion, gratitude, and pride. Here are three activities you and your child can engage in to promote mindfulness.

Gardening

Working the earth and caring for plants is a great way to channel your child's hyperactive tendencies. They're able to move around, dig, weed, water plants, and harvest. Gardening is a hands-on activity that allows your child to move from one task to another. It helps build their self-esteem as they feel they are doing something important. Gardening also reinforces patience as your child awaits the fruits of their labor. As flowers and plants do appear, their pride is further built up. Caring for plants can also build empathy.

Arts and Crafts

Drawing, coloring, and creating things are great mindful activities for your child. They're able to express themselves creatively in ways they may be unable to do verbally. It keeps their hands and minds occupied and allows them to channel their thoughts to create things that represent how they think and feel. Drawing can be a calming, soothing activity. Your child will also feel a sense of pride when viewing their creations. Make sure to praise your child's artwork and display it in your home for other family members to see.

Attention Games

You can engage your child in games that help them to observe their environment. This can be as challenging as you want. Making it a competition can further interest and motivate your child. Since these games are verbal, they can be done in almost any environment. By challenging your child to pick out things like a specific color, shape, object, word, emotion, or person, you're helping them to be more aware of their environment.

SUMMARY

Your child's brain develops differently from the neurotypical brain. They feel things more intensely and these feelings last longer. Your child may experience emotional dysregulation where they have trouble processing their emotions and coming up with an appropriate response. They may experience difficulties in getting motivated, handling stressful situations, and calming themselves down. Your child will give in to impulses and take risks. Their working memory is impaired, preventing them from stepping back and looking at things from different perspectives. Their strongest emotion takes over, and they react without thinking.

You can help your child manage their emotions by teaching them emotional regulation skills. This can be done by encouraging them to stop and think, accept and face stressful situations, and come up with solutions to problems. After providing your child with techniques and helping them to practice, you should take a step back and let them try them on their own. It is important to remain patient and not be discouraged when your child takes a bit longer to learn how to handle their emotions. Building their emotional vocabulary, acknowledging their feelings, and allowing them to express themselves will help develop their emotional intelligence.

It is important to teach your child gratitude, pride, and empathy. This can be done by modeling these emotions for your child, expressing thanks, and helping others. You can create activities and visual reminders geared toward helping your child build those three prosocial emotions.

A frustration log will help you keep track of and identify your child's behavioral patterns and triggers. Practicing mindfulness through games, gardening, and arts and crafts will also help your child manage their intense emotions. As your child develops their emotional regulation skills, they become better able to create and maintain relationships. In the next chapter, we will focus on your child's social skills.

7

MAKING FRIENDS

My daughter was an awkward child. She would sail out into the world with the best intentions and crash into the iceberg known as making friends. She wanted to make friends, and she did, but the nuances of communicating with others would trip her up. After doing some research, I learned that I could not simply open my door and nudge her out into the friendship pool. She had to learn the things spoken about in the previous chapter, like emotional regulation, compassion, and empathy. These things helped build her social skills and improved her interactions with others. They are the foundation of effective communication.

ADHD AND YOUR CHILD'S SOCIAL DEVELOPMENT

Communication is both verbal and nonverbal. Our body language and gestures say just as much as our speech. Your child's ADHD symptoms interfere with how your child communicates. When your child is hyperactive, they will have rapid speech, scattered thoughts, become hyper-focused on specific points, and constantly interrupt others. Their inattentiveness can result in them becoming overwhelmed and withdrawing into themselves. They will miss parts of conversations and social cues. Sounds in their environment will easily distract them, and they will find it difficult to listen to others. Your child's impulsivity can cause them to invade people's personal spaces, act goofy, try to start conversations during inappropriate moments, and show aggression.

Waiting their turn and managing their emotions is challenging during social interactions. Their tendency to be distracted or take over conversations can push people away. Your child can become frustrated and avoid socializing. This creates a difficult cycle where your child is unable to practice and develop their social skills through much-needed interaction.

Building relationships with peers teaches you cooperation, negotiation, and problem-solving. It provides different perspectives and helps you learn from others. Social groups provide a much-needed sense of belonging and acceptance. Socializing teaches you to accept the differences of others and navigate conflict. It also builds empathy.

Interaction Between Your Child's Academic Achievements and Social Skills

Being able to control and regulate your emotions and actions affects how you perform in school. The symptoms of ADHD make this difficult for your child. Your child might struggle with asking for help and completing activities. Sports and group collaboration may also be difficult, as are class discussions and presentations. You can help your child overcome these challenges by practicing with them at home and teaching them the things outlined in the previous chapter.

IMPROVING YOUR CHILD'S SOCIAL SKILLS

Your child looks to you to provide them with the extra steps they need to bridge the gap between themselves and others. You can help your child by having a discussion with them on the need to develop their skills so that they can become better communicators. Let them know that improving their social skills is important as it will improve their friendships. In working on these skills, start small and be specific. Work towards one clear goal at a time. Allow your child opportunities to practice what they have learned by arranging supervised playdates with a specific start and end time. Keep the activities in these playdates simple but fun, and end the playdate positively. Keep in mind your child's hyperactivity and limited attention span and plan accordingly. You can record your child when they're engaging in various activities. You can then watch these recordings with your child and discuss their strengths and areas for improvement. This will help them become more self-aware so that they can self-regulate. You can also help your child by making verbal observations of what others might be feeling based on their expressions and body language. As mentioned in the previous chapter, building your child's empathy will also build their social skills.

Consider your child's triggers when working on their social skills. What caused their behavior? How did they react? How do we work on this for next time? Provide simple, direct instructions and model the desired behavior. If you have observed, for example, a game where your child always has an outburst, practice this game with them and work on their behavior. Find children who may share similarities to your child and will likely understand them. Help your child read social cues and with self-reflection. This is important as your child does not always know what others are feeling or understand their responses. Increasing their social awareness will improve their interactions.

Keep providing feedback to your child. Help them learn how to start conversations, wait their turn before speaking, respect personal space, and show interest in the thoughts and feelings of the other person. Help your child practice these skills over and over again. You can remain involved in helping develop your child's friendships and introducing them to peers as they get older. Just remember that teenagers and young adults value their independence. Consider your child's feelings when helping develop these friendships. Involve the school in your efforts. Partner with them in improving your child's peer interactions at school. You can help create a classroom that is ADHD friendly and work out strategies with your child's teacher that will help manage your child's symptoms. We will look more at ADHD in school in the next chapter.

HOW TO MAKE FRIENDS

You can help your child understand the values of friendship and social interaction. Start by listening to your child, understanding them, and having meaningful discussions with them. Become your child's first friend. Praise your child's strengths when you see them interacting with others, but also offer gentle criticism. Correct any observed negative behaviors. Help your child make choices in how to communicate with others. You can put yourself in situations—by volunteering at their school or arranging playdates—where you can observe their interactions. You can then help your child understand the social cues and appropriate responses. Remember the importance of planning and structuring social activities for your child. It's also important to match your level of supervision to your child's age. They may need more hands-on help when they are younger, but you should try to recognize when it's time to stand back and let them apply what you have taught them. Have a chat session with your child after playdates and other social events to discuss what happened, how they felt, and what can be improved.

You can help your child develop their social skills by engaging them in team sports and activities. This gives them a chance to practice working with others toward a shared goal. Your child will learn the value of meeting the needs of the team rather than just considering themselves. Before signing your child up for team activities, talk to the coach about expectations. Find out if the team is ADHD-friendly and arrange for your child to meet the coach and teammates beforehand in a situation where you can provide support if needed. If your child's competitive streak makes things difficult, try engaging them in sports or activities where they can perform on their own. Their efforts will still count towards the overall score of the team.

Your worry is understandable but remind yourself that your child will be okay. With your guidance, they will eventually find their footing. You can find a mentor to help guide your child. This mentor may be able to interact with your child in ways that you may not. This could be because of where the mentor is able to interact with the child, or simply because sometimes, your child is more receptive to things that don't come from you. It's okay if your child doesn't have an abundance of friends. Having even one close friend will be of great benefit. Seek out children with similar hobbies as these shared interests can help form a connection that can lead to friendship.

Start small with playdates. One-on-one interactions can help ease your child into building relationships with others. Eventually, you can invite more children. Your child's level of maturity may be below their age. As a result, they might be more comfortable interacting with children younger than they are. Set an example for your child by being involved in community ventures and social activities. This will show your child how to behave, as well as the importance of building and maintaining connections with others. Teach your child to stand up to bullying while remembering to self-regulate so that they do not overreact. Step back as your child gets older and allow them to sort out situations on their own. You can still keep an eye on them but allow them to take charge of their own socializing. Think about using medication to help manage your child's symptoms while they're interacting with others. Work with your healthcare provider and your child to ensure that the dosage is correct.

I SAY, YOU SAY

You can use this game to help your child understand that conversation involves taking turns.

You: I say, 'Good morning,' you say…?

Child: Good morning

You: I say, 'How are you?' You say…?

Child: I am fine, and how are you?

Ask questions to help keep the conversation moving. Provide your child with conversation starters like greetings and inquiring after someone's health, family, or day. Teach your child how to extend conversations by asking about the other person's interests, which can help build a connection over shared experiences. Point out and demonstrate eye contact, gestures, expressions, and other body language. Teach them to moderate their tone. Help your child develop their listening skills and show them how to provide verbal and nonverbal cues to let the person know that they are paying attention. These cues could be nodding or saying 'really?' and other such expressions.

You: I say, 'Hello, did you enjoy school today?' You say…?

Child: I say, 'School was fun, but I fell on the playground.' You say…?

You: 'Oh dear, I'm sorry you fell. Are you okay?' You say…?

Child: I am okay, thank you for asking.

(Maguire, 2021).

SUMMARY

Understanding social cues and creating and maintaining friendships can be difficult for your child. Their inability to completely understand some verbal and nonverbal communication can lead them to become frustrated and isolate themselves. This can affect your child's performance at school.

You can help your child by teaching them the importance of making connections with their peers. Doing so will help them learn to negotiate, work as a team, and problem solve. It will also give them a sense of belonging. Discussing the value of friendship with your child and providing a model for them to follow is important. You can schedule timed playdates, pair them with children slightly younger than they are, and discuss each playdate once it is finished. You can also set clear, specific goals and work toward them one at a time.

Consider your child's triggers and come up with strategies to help them. Teach them to stand up to bullies while maintaining their composure. Allow your child to practice, and to see you practicing, all the skills you're teaching them. Engage them in team sports, and work with the coach and teacher to provide an ADHD-friendly environment for them. Provide as much feedback as you can. Play games that show them how to start and maintain conversations, how to read social cues, and how to take turns when speaking.

Building your child's social skills will help them interact with their teachers and peers at school. In the next chapter, we will look at your child's ADHD and how it affects them going to school.

8

GOING TO SCHOOL WITH ADHD

Sometimes it felt like I saw my daughter's middle school and her teachers more than she did. Her work was often incomplete, her desk was messy, and she acted out during recess. The amount of money I spent replacing her lost school items was significant. One day I got called in to see my proud, disheveled girl sitting outside the principal's office. Another child had been mean, and my daughter had reacted with her fists. My daughter was unrepentant. As far as she was concerned, the other girl had started it, and it was unfair that the teachers were being so hard on her. We had a long talk about appropriate reactions. The principal had been ready to bring the hammer down, but after listening to our conversation, he was more lenient. Both she and the other party to the fight received a fair and equal punishment.

Her teacher struggled to get her to take notes. Something always distracted her, or she got frustrated and gave up. Sometimes her name had to be called over and over again to gain her attention. One time the teacher almost had a heart attack when she looked around and discovered my daughter had vanished from the classroom. They found her roaming the school grounds, touching everything and singing to herself.

One thing I admired about her school was that they did not just call me about the struggles. They called me when she achieved goals and displayed positive behavior. We were able to exclaim together in wonder at her stories and art projects. The teacher called her her "little helper" because she was always ready to fetch, arrange, and generally help out. "Your daughter never gives up," they would tell me. It always made me so proud.

Not all the students and parents were kind. Some got frustrated with her, and others did not understand. The school tried its best to make accommodations for her. Her teachers made sure to educate her classmates, hold discussions with me, and implement strategies to help her succeed. Not all teachers were so understanding, but by and large, my daughter's middle school experience was a positive one.

That may not be the case for everyone. As a parent of a child with ADHD, it's natural to worry about how your child will manage at school. People can and will be cruel. Schools may be unwilling to make the accommodations. But that is a trial you and your child can overcome. An ADHD diagnosis in no way prevents your child from going to school. Of children aged 6-11 who attend school, 2.4 million—9.6%—have been diagnosed with ADHD. Many of the famous persons mentioned in previous chapters went to school. They all turned out to be brilliant actors, musicians, athletes, and so much more (ADDtitude Editors, 2022).

ADHD AND THE CLASSROOM

You have read about the symptoms of ADHD in previous chapters. Your child's hyperactivity, impulsiveness, and inattention can interfere with how they learn at school. Symptoms of inattention at school include careless mistakes when doing schoolwork, distraction, incomplete assignments and activities, and trouble following instructions. It also includes trouble organizing tasks and possessions, constant loss of personal items, and difficulty listening when spoken to directly. Your hyperactive child may fidget, have trouble staying in their seat, and blurt out answers. They will interrupt, and run and climb inappropriately. They're constantly moving, have trouble playing quietly, and are always talking.

A lot of these symptoms are a part of growing up. Some children may be younger than their classmates by a year or more, and this can cause their behavior to be more immature than those they share a classroom with. However, when symptoms persist for more than six months and seriously affect their daily lives, then seeking a diagnosis is recommended.

SETTING UP YOUR CHILD FOR SUCCESS AT SCHOOL

Each state has laws that instruct schools on how to operate regarding children with special needs. Some states require the schools to be inclusive and to provide special programs to help these students. Some organizations cater specifically to educating those with special needs. Keep up to date on the laws and resources relevant to your state. Have discussions with the teacher on your child's symptoms, personality, and the strategies you're using. Each child is unique, so telling the teacher about your child's strengths and areas of improvement will help that teacher create plans specific to your child. Make a request to the school that accommodations be put in place for your child. These can include special breaks or the use of interactive multimedia. Presenting lessons in a way suited to your child's learning style will help to keep them engaged in class. Ask the teacher to consider your child's needs when making seating arrangements. Some areas of the classroom may be less distracting than others. Your child might also need to take tests and study in distraction-free environments. Where your child sits may detract from or enhance their learning.

Keep an open line of communication between yourself and the school. Discuss changes and suggested improvements in both environments. However, remember to put a boundary in place on how much you will interfere in your child's life. While they need your support, their independence is also important. Organization begins at home. Set up routines and visual aids to help your child organize themselves. Charts, logs, checklists, games, and audio-visual cues can all be used to help guide your child. If you practice organization at home, your child will practice it at school as well with the help of the teacher. The constant change in activities and environments at school can be quite challenging for your child. You can help them by creating tools and strategies to deal with the changes. Practice switching subjects and changing rooms with your child at home. You can also try to get lesson activities and key terms beforehand and go over them with your child.

Working With Your Child's Teacher

Teachers have a lot to handle between lesson plans, meetings, and managing entire classrooms of students. You can help your child and their teacher by planning regular meetings to discuss your child. You can pre-schedule these meetings to occur monthly or any period of time that is agreed upon by you and the teacher. Once the schedule has been agreed upon, stick to it. Try to make these meetings as much as possible. Having meetings in the classroom will give you a chance to familiarize yourself with the area your child learns in. Work with your child's teacher to create goals, and plan the strategies and steps that will be taken to reach those goals. Make sure these goals are realistic and attainable within an agreed timeframe.

Give the teacher as much information as you can. Tell them about your child's history, triggers, and anything you think might be useful. You should also listen carefully to any information the teacher shares. You may not always hear what you want to hear, but denial will not help your child. Do not be afraid to ask about the problems your child has been experiencing at school. Tell the teacher about any medications or treatments your child is undergoing.

Managing ADHD at School

▷ **Distractibility**

Your child's teacher can help keep them focused by allowing breaks and cutting large tasks into smaller ones. The teacher can shift between seated and moving activities. They can ensure the child is not seated close to windows and doors where they can be distracted by things happening outside. Information can be written down for the child to reference when needed, and the teacher can remind the student to check this information.

▷ **Impulsiveness**

If your child displays negative behavior, the necessary discipline should be carried out immediately. In doing so, the teacher ensures that the child knows exactly why they are being disciplined. The teacher should also provide verbal praise and acknowledgment when your child achieves a goal or does something well. The teacher can create and put up a daily plan of activities. Each activity can be crossed off as they are completed. A behavior plan can also be created and placed within the child's view.

▷ **Interrupting**

Your child may be prone to interruption without realizing the effect it can have on classroom activities. Your child's teacher can address this privately without calling the child out in front of the entire classroom, as this can be embarrassing. Instead, you, the teacher, and your child can work out signals and gestures. When these gestures are made, the child will realize that they should raise their hands or wait their turn. When activities are completed without interruptions, the child should be praised.

▷ **Difficulty Following Instructions**

Your child's teacher can use scaffolding, social stories, and videos to help guide your child in understanding instructions. These instructions should be brief, specific, and clear. The teacher can write down instructions and add extra steps to reinforce lesson content for your child. A firm, calm tone should be used to remind and redirect your child whenever they veer off course.

▷ **Hyperactivity and Fidgeting**

Your child's screen time can be limited, and they can instead be encouraged to engage in physical activities. Toys that can be squeezed, spun, and otherwise manipulated can also be provided. This can help your child move their hands while remaining seated. Your child's teacher can also send them to run errands around the school. This gives them a chance to get up and move in a meaningful way.

Making Reading Fun

Reading is an important skill for anyone to learn. However, it does require a lot of sitting and concentrating. This might be difficult for your child. Thankfully, there are many ways that you and your child's teacher can make reading fun. Putting aside time for family reading with your child can help interest them in books. You can take turns selecting the stories to read. You and your child can take turns picking a character to act out and pretend to be. Changing your voices and using props and costumes can help bring the characters to life. You can keep your child engaged by playing guessing games and making predictions on what happens next. Make it a competition to see who turns out to be right.

Making Math Fun

You can make math fun by using concrete objects that your child can manipulate. This will help them understand abstract concepts. You can also use cards, dice, and other games to interest your child. Songs, jingles, and poems can also be created to help your child make associations. These associations will aid them in learning terms and remembering how to do mathematical operations. Pictures can also be used to help your child understand math concepts.

Managing Homework

You can help your child with their homework by creating a scheduled time when it is to be done and working with them in a distraction-free environment. Use clocks and watches to monitor the time and work in 10–20-minute intervals with breaks in between. You and your child's teacher can schedule a time when homework is handed directly to the teacher. This homework can be placed in a specific part of your child's bag for them to easily access and remember. Create a homework folder to store all assignments and any papers and tools related to homework. Teach your child how to organize this folder. You can keep copies of notes and textbooks at home if possible. Work daily with your child to organize all their school items. Checklists can be used to ensure that your child has completed the necessary tasks and has the necessary items. Encourage proper sleep, exercise, and healthy eating. Remember to take care of yourself so you can take care of your child.

SCHOOL STRATEGIES

In addition to the strategies mentioned above, there are several other things your child's teacher can do to manage their symptoms. The teacher can arrange for other members of staff, older students, and others to mentor and provide additional support for your child. If your child is being paired with another student, the teacher should ensure that this student is understanding, mature, and willing to help. This student can study with your child and provide reminders about lessons and assignments. The teacher can also arrange to have the more challenging lessons during periods where your child is known to regularly be engaged and paying attention. Your child can also be allowed to stand when completing certain tasks or engaging in some activities. While school rules are to be obeyed, some flexibility can be allowed for your child within reason. Rewards can be varied to keep your child interested. Your child's teacher should keep in mind that limiting activities like recess and sports may not be the best. In doing so, they are closing off an avenue for your child to direct their energy by playing.

SUMMARY

Your child's ADHD symptoms can affect their academic performance. There are several tools and strategies you can use to help set your child up for academic success. You can talk to your child's teacher, create a daily report card, schedule regular meetings, and plan strategies together. Your child's school may be willing to make accommodations based on your child's needs. States have different requirements about how children with special needs should be educated, and being aware of these requirements can be very helpful. You can model behaviors and practice transition and organization strategies at home. Maintain communication with your child's teacher. Share your child's strengths and weaknesses and listen carefully to what the teacher has to say about your child.

Your child's tendency to be easily distracted can be managed by changing where they sit, alternating standing and seated activities, and making accommodations for where tests are held. Their hyperactivity can be managed by giving them errands, limiting screen time, providing manipulatable objects, and engaging your child in a sport. Impulsivity can be aided by applying immediate consequences to behavior, praising good behavior out loud, and placing schedules and behavior plans where the child can see them.

You can help your child enjoy reading and mathematics through the use of games, daily stories, manipulatable objects, roleplays, and drawings. Encouraging proper sleep, exercise, and diet will also help your child perform better at school. You can help your child with their homework by doing it at a scheduled time in a distraction-free environment. Homework and studying can be broken into smaller parts with breaks in between.

At school, your child's teacher should have clear, consistent expectations, provide constant feedback, and arrange for support where necessary. At home, you can help your child by establishing daily routines, which we will discuss in the next chapter.

9

DAILY ROUTINES

I was well aware that routines were an important part of raising children with ADHD. However, that point was driven home to me one day when I came home exhausted from a long day at work. In no time at all, I fell asleep. I was not happy when I was shaken awake by my daughter, who insisted it was time for one of our conversation games. To me, it was something simple that could be done at another time. I tried to send her on her way because I was so tired, and it was not fair for me to get up and do this with her when she had so many toys to occupy her. She left unhappy, and I tried to go back to sleep. Guilt soon drove me from my bed in search of my child. I found her unhappily but obediently playing with her toys. Her face lit up when I told her we could play her game after all. What was, to me, a simple thing was so much more to her.

Your child is easily distracted, and their thoughts are constantly pulling at them. Having a predictable environment helps them feel safe and makes it easier for them to focus and self-regulate. You can help your child by establishing morning, after school, dinner, and bedtime routines. Children with ADHD have difficulty with school, relationships, and even their self-esteem. Studies have shown that structure helps minimize their symptoms and lessens the chance of outbursts and rebellion. Your child is better able to cope and manage their symptoms.

Morning routines can include showering, brushing their teeth, exchanging greetings with family members, and eating breakfast. You can make your morning routines more manageable by preparing for them the night before. Reduce distractions and check in occasionally on your child to make sure they're on track.

School can be exhausting, and having after-school routines can help your child unwind and settle in for the rest of the afternoon at home. You can supervise your child, provide healthy snacks, and assist them with their homework and assignments.

Dinnertime routines can help your family communicate about each other's days over a meal. A good night's rest is very important, and you can help your child settle in for the night by creating a routine that may include showering, brushing their teeth, a few minutes of screen time, a bedtime story, and more.

ADHD, SCHEDULES, AND STRUCTURE

Providing structure and predictability can help reduce conflicts at home. It provides external stimuli that can help your child to regulate themselves by following a routine. Routines can apply to the whole family, which will help your child feel included and help build relationships between family members. It helps your child develop habits and behavior patterns toward chores and activities. These habits will be beneficial to your child as they grow into adulthood. All these serve to help your child achieve success by having a firm foundation provided for them in the home.

When creating an ADHD-friendly schedule, be specific about what is expected and the steps that are to be taken with chores and activities. Provide limited choices to prevent your child from being overwhelmed by options. Allow for periods of physical activity to help your child manage their impulsivity and hyperactivity. Visual cues can help provide a focused reminder on what your child is expected to do and how they're expected to behave. You can involve your child in the process by having them choose an activity they would like to do. Having some level of flexibility is required as sometimes adjustments have to be made to the schedule.

CREATING ADHD-FRIENDLY ROUTINES

The most common types of routines are ones that focus on discipline, the household, and homework.

Household Routines

There are several routines that can provide structure to your family. These include

- taking out the garbage on specific days
- recycling
- washing dishes after each meal
- family games night
- family meetings
- allotted screen time
- volunteering
- scheduled time for household chores
- scheduled time for family outings
- putting away toys not in use

- taking care of pets and plants at designated times
- scheduled time to read stories or listen to calming music before bed

Homework Routines

Homework routines can include

- taking breaks every 10–20 minutes
- organizing homework materials
- removing distractions from homework area
- using quizzes or games
- working with other family members
- using a checklist to keep track of assignments

Discipline Routines

Establishing clear discipline routines can help manage behaviors and decrease conflict. These include

- creating clear, simple family rules and outlining disciplinary actions that will be taken when the rules are broken
- setting the number of times your child will receive a warning before stricter discipline is applied

- encouraging apologies and showing forgiveness through verbal acceptance and hugs
- holding family discussions on how certain behaviors should be dealt with
- applying discipline immediately following the negative behavior
- keeping disciplinary actions fair and equal to the misbehavior
- being consistent in applying discipline
- following through on any disciplinary action you say you will do

BEING STRICT BUT FLEXIBLE

Being consistent and staying true to your word is an important part of applying effective discipline. However, rigid adherence can lead to feelings of resentment and worsening ADHD symptoms. Take each situation on a case-by-case basis and consider the circumstances. Encourage your child to express themselves in a respectful manner. You can make additions to specific rules when needed. Changes can be made as a reward and acknowledgment of good behavior. Keep these changes within a specific parameter. For example, you can allow your child a choice in scheduled activities. They may be required to eat a healthy snack at noon, but they can choose what that snack is.

PROVIDING DISCIPLINE FOR YOUR MISBEHAVING CHILD

In enforcing discipline, it's essential that you accept your child for who they are and understand that with ADHD comes certain symptoms. No child is perfect, and certain behaviors will pop up as they grow and learn about themselves and the world. However, you should also be careful about believing every negative thing someone tells you about your child. Talk to your child and allow them to explain themselves. Also, consider the source of the information you're receiving. It's important to listen and acknowledge that your child has misbehaved rather than blaming everyone around the child. Use disciplinary actions and intervention strategies instead of solely relying on medication. Medication helps manage symptoms, but it does not mean that your child doesn't need additional guidance.

In your desire to help your child be their best selves, make sure you're not just punishing them all the time. Punishment involves forcing your child to behave a certain way by applying negative stimuli. Discipline is showing your child how to behave. With discipline, you provide alternatives and explain what changes the child needs to make and why. Some persistent behavior requires punishment, but it should never be in the form of any type of physical or verbal abuse.

Just because your child does something 'bad' doesn't mean they are bad. Be careful about making associations between the action and the child. Also, try not to discipline your child for behaviors they cannot control. Instead, use tools and strategies to help guide them in how to manage their behavior. Try not to say no to everything your child asks. Instead, listen and then make decisions based on the situation. You can also explain why you're saying no.

Focus on your child's areas of strength. Do not simply overwhelm them with negative criticisms. Give rewards and verbal acknowledgment for the completion of tasks and for displays of positive behaviors. Plan ahead for potential negative behaviors. Being prepared can help how you react and how the child learns the consequences of their actions. Don't be afraid to seek outside help. Sometimes you're unable to manage on your own, and that's okay. Talk to other family members, your child's teacher, and your healthcare professional.

Try to remain calm and use a firm tone when disciplining your child. Stop and take deep breaths if you feel emotionally overwhelmed. Do not engage in fights with your children. If you have to get outside and take a walk, do so. A change in environment for you and your child can help. When applying time-outs, the length of time should be equal to the crime. You can also point out the positive behavior the child was engaged in before the misbehavior.

Use scaffolding and take the extra steps necessary to provide your child with the tools and strategies necessary to manage their behavior. Keep your expectations consistent with your child's capabilities and level of maturity. Use clear, specific instructions. You can break the day into parts and offer rewards when the goal for each part has been achieved. Find your child's triggers and remove them from the environment, along with things that may be overly distracting. When your child encounters a challenge and has a strong reaction, redirect them by offering alternatives.

Make sure that your child is aware of the rules, rewards, disciplinary actions, and expectations. Your child is more likely to remember and stick to rules they help create, so involve them in the rule-making process. Apply discipline for misbehavior in the moment, not after the fact. Avoid embarrassing them in front of others when applying discipline. Be consistent and honest with yourself, and practice and model self-discipline. You can use the token system where your child receives tokens when they meet specific goals. After a certain amount of tokens have been collected, your child can trade them in for a reward. When you're praising your child, tell them exactly what the positive behavior is rather than generalizing.

TAKING A DEEPER LOOK AT ROUTINES AND ADHD

When creating a routine, consider what you want your child to be in the future. Look at where your child is now, and create steps to help them become more independent and to achieve success. If your child struggles with reaching a larger goal, break it into smaller goals and celebrate the achievement of each one. Involve your child in the creation and implementation of routines, rewards, and discipline. Ask questions that prompt them to think of solutions to different situations. Do not try to tackle all behaviors at once. Work a little at a time; be patient and encouraging. If you find that a routine is too stressful, slow it down and make adjustments. Rather than only looking at the negative behaviors you want to change, focus more on the positive behaviors you want your child to exhibit.

ROUTINES FOR YOUR CHILD

Daily structure and predictability can make your child more efficient and productive while building family bonds. Keeping to a routine requires a lot of commitment. Do not be discouraged or give up. Encourage and offer support to any and all family members who are struggling with the routines.

Morning Routine

Set a specific time for family members to wake up. You can gradually start the process of waking your child a few minutes earlier than the specified wake-up time to ensure they are alert. Prepare for morning routines the night before and try to eliminate distractions that will interfere with the routine. Breakfast is the most important meal of the day and should be the main priority of the morning routine. Divide morning tasks among family members to avoid overcrowding in areas like the bathroom. Try to start the morning with a smile and a calm demeanor. Keep your weekdays and weekend mornings the same for consistency. As always, provide rewards for good behavior.

Homework Routine

As previously mentioned, setting a consistent time will help your child. Taking breaks, closely supervising your child, and having fun once all homework is complete will also provide a helpful routine.

Dinner Routine

Keep a consistent schedule for dinner. Encourage the family to sit and eat together without devices. Model conversation starters and extenders. Discuss events and listen to what everyone has to say. Assign roles to your child, such as setting and clearing the table.

Bedtime Routine

You can help your child wind down with a story, calm music, or a quiet game. Create and keep nightly rituals such as saying a prayer, quote, or poem, or giving hugs and kisses. You can allow your child to have a light, healthy snack. Try to keep to a scheduled and consistent bedtime.

SAMPLE SCHEDULE

7:00 am—Gently wake your child
7:02 am—Begin the morning with a positive motivational quote, poem, or song
7:08 am—Start the morning ritual of washing face, showering, combing hair, getting dressed, etc.
7:30 am—Go to the kitchen for a healthy breakfast. Exchange morning greetings, discuss plans for the day and offer suggestions.

7:55 am—Brush teeth, put on any remaining clothes items, grab school items

8:10 am—Leave the house

3:00 pm—Greet everyone, have a light snack, and discuss your day

3:30 pm—Begin homework

3:45 pm—Take a break

4:00 pm—Resume homework

4:15 pm—Another break

4:30 pm—Complete homework

4:30 pm–5:30 pm—Play activities, including screen time

5:30 pm—Dinner prep, including setting the table

6:30 pm—Dinner time

7:15 pm—Clear the table and wash dishes

7:25 pm–7:55 pm—Family discussion and games

8:00 pm—Bath time, brushing of teeth, and changing into night clothes

8:30 pm—Storytime

8:45 pm—End the night on a positive note and let your child know it is time to sleep

(Jaksa, 2022).

SUMMARY

Routines and structure are important for your child because they help them to self-regulate while handling symptoms of impulsiveness and hyperactivity. Establishing routines helps your child feel safe and secure. It promotes family bonding, fosters independence, and reduces conflicts. Routines provide a firm foundation for your child and help develop positive habits. You can establish routines for any time of day. For morning routines, prep the night before, provide a healthy breakfast, and supervise your child as they get ready. After school, you can create routines that help your child with their homework and prepare them for dinner. Routines at night help your child unwind and rest for the challenges of the next day.

Discipline helps your child exhibit positive behaviors and decreases negative behaviors. Be firm, calm, and flexible when disciplining your child. Apply discipline immediately, establish rules and consequences, and be consistent. Accept your child for who they are, and do not believe every bad thing you hear about them. Praise positive behaviors and redirect your child when necessary. Don't confuse punishment with discipline, and ask for outside help when you need it.

Your child is a superstar, and with proper guidance, they will shine. Understanding what ADHD is, its symptoms, and what a diagnosis means will help you in accepting your child for who they are. It will help you in deciding on the treatment you want to pursue—whether it be medication, behavioral therapy, or both. With this firm foundation, you'll be able to teach your child how to manage their intense emotions and how to make friends. It will help you in working with the school to provide support for your child and make you better equipped to create daily routines and structure. This book seeks to provide you with these foundations and equip you with these skills. The story of my experiences with my child and the research I have done will guide you down the path to a better future for you and your child. Thank you for going on this journey with me to the very end. Your child is incredible, and so are you for doing everything you can to understand them.

CONCLUSION

Learning about your child's brain will help you to understand why they are the way they are. Attention Deficit Hyperactivity Disorder (ADHD) begins in childhood and presents symptoms of inattention, hyperactivity, and impulsiveness. These symptoms affect your child's daily life. The structure of the ADHD brain is different from that of the neurotypical brain. It is smaller, and some parts are under- or overactive. The brain also matures at a slower rate. Brain chemicals like norepinephrine and dopamine are not as plentiful. This affects emotions, habit formation, attention span, and decision-making. Once you're aware of the function and structure of the ADHD brain, you can gain an insight into your child's symptoms. These symptoms include fidgeting, the inability to follow instructions, lack of focus, and being unable to sit still. Your child will act without thinking and move as if operated by a powerful motor. They may daydream, lose things, and lack organizational and social skills. They take risks, invade personal space, and leave assignments unfinished.

If your child presents six or more symptoms of ADHD for more than six months, they may be diagnosed with ADHD by a trained professional. The criteria for this diagnosis can be found in the DSM-5 manual. There are many conditions that can be mistaken for ADHD. These include depression, bipolar disorder, autism spectrum disorder, Tourette's syndrome, conduct disorders, obsessive-compulsive disorder, and others. If you feel your child is misdiagnosed, talk to a professional.

Receiving a diagnosis can be challenging. You may feel lost and not know what step to take. An important step is accepting your child and teaching them to accept themselves. There are individuals and organizations that work to raise ADHD awareness, and you can do so too. Your child has superpowers. They are creative, empathic, enthusiastic, and so much more. With proper guidance, these skills can help them succeed in life.

There are several medical and non-medical treatments for ADHD. Each individual has a unique reaction to medication, and the dosage and type of medication is recommended on an individual basis.

You and your child may benefit greatly from behavioral therapy, which can be used alongside or instead of medication.

Your child feels things more intensely than the average person. You can help your child manage their emotions by teaching them the prosocial behaviors of gratitude, pride, and empathy. Model and practice these skills and provide feedback for your child. Not only do they help your child regulate their emotions, but they also enhance their social skills.

Your child may have difficulty making friends due to their ADHD symptoms. You can help by modeling social behaviors and teaching them social cues. Offer gentle criticism and positive feedback and play games that help them navigate social situations. Be your child's friendship coach. You can arrange playdates but remember to respect your child's independence as they grow older.

There is a lot you can do to help your child succeed at school and at home. You can work with your child's teacher to promote positive behavior and keep rules and rewards consistent. Accommodations can be made to introduce strategies suited to your child's learning style and to help them take tests in distraction-free environments. Setting up daily morning, after school, homework, dinner, and bedtime activities provide consistency and structure for your child. It helps them to feel calm and to self-regulate in a controlled environment.

My daughter is now a blossoming high school student and already dreams of going to college. It has been a joy to see her embrace herself as the brilliant, independent woman she is meant to be. Looking back, I see the struggles clearly. The changes in school, therapists, and medications. The countless nights and constant research. Every moment was worth it. There were also so many highs. My daughter and I have learned so much about life and each other. We have motivated, inspired, and helped each other to grow.

It has been a pleasure to share my story with you. You are not alone, and I know you and your child will move on to great things. There will be challenges, but with love, patience, and the methods you have learned in this book, your child will grow up to be the best version of themselves.

Help me reach more parents like us by leaving a review on Amazon.

And while we are here…

Take a deep breath.

Smile.

Say to yourself, "I love my awesome, incredible child, and I know I will be the parent they need. I may stumble, but I will never stop and never fall."

Wishing you the best of luck on your journey,

Lydia.

LEAVE A QUICK REVIEW!

Thank you for choosing this book to learn more about parenting your child with ADHD. My daughter and I put a lot of time, research, and emotional labor into making this book as helpful as possible for families like ours. If you enjoyed this book, please consider leaving us an Amazon review with your honest feedback. Reviews help us reach more readers and improve our future projects! We look forward to reading your thoughts.

For readers in the US:

For readers in Canada:

For readers in the UK:

GLOSSARY

Accommodations: This is when a school adjusts its curriculum and strategies to help children with special needs. Accommodations include changes to the physical space, the way tests are given, the materials used, and the way lesson content is taught.

Acceptance and commitment therapy: Therapy that asks you to confront and accept negative thoughts, identify values, and use the values as a guide through life. It also involves committing to reach set goals.

ADD: Acronym for Attention Deficit Disorder. It refers to ADHD that presents more symptoms of inattention and less hyperactivity.

ADHD: Acronym for Attention-Deficit/Hyperactivity Disorder. This condition presents itself in childhood through adulthood and includes symptoms of hyperactivity, impulsiveness, and inattention. ADHD affects how people behave and can interfere with their daily life.

ADHD coach: A trained professional who mainly helps older teens and adults to master their ADHD symptoms and achieve their goals.

ADHD-Combined: The most common type of ADHD where a child presents all the symptoms of hyperactivity, impulsiveness, and inattention.

ADHD-Not Otherwise Specified: A subtype of ADHD in which the child presents symptoms from the three groups (hyperactivity, impulsiveness, and inattention). These symptoms do not fully match the criteria for the other types of ADHD.

ADHD-Hyperactive-Impulsive: A type of ADHD where the child presents symptoms of hyperactivity and impulsiveness with limited symptoms of inattention.

ADHD-Inattentive: Also referred to as ADD (see above).

Anxiety: Fear and worry about daily life. This fear can overtake the mind and impair daily function. Anxiety and ADHD sometimes occur together.

Attentional bias: When someone chooses to pay attention to the things they find interesting instead of things that are not as engaging.

Aversion therapy: Therapy used to help your child create negative associations for pleasurable but unhealthy behavior.

Basal ganglia: Part of the brain that helps control voluntary movement.

Behavioral contract: A contract that outlines expected positive behavior, along with the rewards for this behavior. This contract is made between parent and child or student and teacher.

Behavioral therapy: Therapy used to treat various mental disorders by helping individuals to self-evaluate themselves, identify negative thoughts, and promote positive thinking. This allows them to change undesirable behaviors.

Child behavior checklist: A checklist that is rated on a scale. It is used to evaluate a child's behavioral patterns.

Classroom behavior management: These are the tools and strategies that teachers use to manage students' behavior in the classroom.

Clinical trial: A research study used to test a new approach, intervention, or treatment.

Co-existing conditions: Two or more mental health conditions that occur at the same time within an individual.

Cognitive behavioral therapy: Therapy that focuses on identifying and changing negative thought patterns to positive ones.

Cognitive behavioral play therapy: Therapy where a child is asked to play while being observed by a therapist. This observation helps the therapist identify areas of comfort and discomfort.

Cognitive restructuring: Making changes to negative thought patterns that have been created by experiences in early life.

Comorbidity: Two or more disorders occurring in an individual at the same time.

Comprehensive assessment: A thorough evaluation of factors that affect a person's difficulties including looking at family history, recent events, trauma, medical conditions, abilities and strengths, and more.

Conduct disorder: Lack of impulse control in children and adolescents which results in aggressive and illegal behavior.

Daily behavior report card: A method used by both parent and teacher to track a child's daily positive and negative behaviors and their progress. The teacher marks whether or not the child has achieved a daily goal and the parent administers either a reward or discipline.

Diagnostic and Statistical Manual of Mental Disorders: This was written by the American Psychiatric Association. It is a manual that outlines the classification and symptoms of mental health disorders and is used for diagnosis by health professionals.

Dialectical behavioral therapy: When a person is taught coping skills through regulating their emotions, examining their distress tolerance, practicing mindfulness, and working on their interpersonal communications and relationships.

Distractibility: When a person's focus is constantly interrupted by thoughts or external stimuli.

Dopamine: A brain chemical that helps control your movements and promotes habits by making you feel pleasure when doing certain things. It also helps you process information and emotion.

Dyslexia: This learning disability affects how a person reads. It results in difficulties with spelling, choosing the correct word when speaking, and problems with general fluency.

Dysthymia: Depression that is mild but persistent.

Emotional dysregulation: The inability to control your emotions.

Executive function: Daily tasks carried out by the brain that help people effectively perform tasks and interact with their environment.

Free appropriate public education: The Individuals with Disabilities Education Act (IDEA) and Rehabilitation Act of 1973 has a Section 504 provision that states that all children have a right to free, appropriate public education that is designed to meet the needs of both neurotypical children, and children with special needs.

Functional impairment difficulties: These are challenges that interfere with a person's ability to function in major life activities, including social situations, school, employment, and in the community.

Hyperactivity: The tendency to be constantly moving, impulsive, and with a limited attention span.

Hyperfocus: Deeply mentally concentrating on one thing.

Impulsivity: The quality of a person who acts based on their whims or immediate thoughts, with no consideration for the consequences and effects of their actions.

Inattention: Not focusing or paying attention to an activity or task.

Independent educational evaluation: This occurs when a qualified professional carries out an assessment designed to see if a child is eligible for special education.

Individualized Education Plan: A plan written by a teacher that outlines the educational goals for an individual student, and the steps that will be taken to achieve these goals.

Individuals with Disabilities Education Act (IDEA): A United States special education law that mandates that all children with special needs from all states should receive free appropriate public education in the "least restrictive environment."

Intervention: A structured plan of action geared toward making changes to an individual's behavior or thought patterns.

Least restrictive environment (LRE): This requires children with special needs to be educated with their neurotypical peers in the same environment. Additional support can be given to students who need it.

Limbic system: Part of the brain that deals with your emotions and behavior. It helps with storing and retrieving memories as well as survival behaviors.

Medication holiday: A scheduled time where a person takes a break from using prescribed medication.

Mental health therapist: Professional counselors, psychologists, psychiatrists, and others who are trained and licensed in assessing, diagnosing, and treating mental health disorders.

Modification: Any adjustments a school system makes to lesson content, curriculum, assignment, or examination to cater to the needs of a student who requires extra support.

Multimodal treatment: Using several methods of treatment and intervention programs simultaneously to help a child with a disability.

Negative self-talk: Thoughts that cause anxiety, anger, and depression, especially during periods of stress.

Neurobehavioral: The connection between the brain and how a person behaves.

Neurodivergent: A person whose brain's structure, development, and function differ from what is considered to be the average for a general population.

Neurologist: Someone who works in the health profession and is trained in diagnosing and treating disorders of the brain.

Neuropsychologist: A trained psychologist who specializes in the effects the brain and nervous system have on a person's thought processes and behavior.

Neurotransmitter: A chemical in the brain that sends messages through the nervous system.

Neurotypical: A person whose brain behaves and functions in a manner that is considered to be the average for a general population.

Non-stimulant medication: Medication used to treat the symptoms of ADHD when stimulant medication cannot be used for health reasons.

Norepinephrine: A stress hormone and brain chemical that helps you pay attention in stressful situations.

Occupational therapist: Someone who is licensed to provide therapy that helps the emotional, physical, and behavioral symptoms of ADHD and helps the child create achievable goals.

Peer rejection: The act of being deliberately excluded from social interactions by one's peers.

Planned ignoring: This behavior intervention strategy advises parents to deliberately ignore negative, attention-seeking behaviors to reduce the behavior(s).

Positive behavioral support: A well-researched plan of action used to increase positive behaviors and phase out negative ones through a systematic approach.

Prefrontal cortex: The part of the frontal lobe in the brain that helps someone to focus and think about the consequences of their actions. It also helps manage impulses and emotions.

Progress monitoring: Continuous assessment of a child's academic performance and how effective the strategies used to teach the child are.

Prosocial behavior: Having the desire and taking action to show empathy, appreciation, and care toward others.

Psychologist: A trained, licensed professional who specializes in emotions, behavior, and how a person functions in their daily life.

Psychoeducational testing: Identifying a child's areas of strengths and weaknesses through various assessments to create an educational plan to help the child.

Rebound effect: The appearance of more serious symptoms when the use of medication has been stopped.

Response to intervention: An intervention program used by schools to promote student success and decrease negative behaviors.

Reticular activating system: Part of the brain that filters out unnecessary information and helps register and organize information.

Scaffolding: Providing temporary support to a child to help them reach a higher level of comprehension and mastery. Assistance is given at the right time and in the right way, with the aim of setting the child up to complete the task independently.

Self-regulation: Adjusting your thought processes, emotion, and behavior to achieve set goals despite challenges and stressful situations.

Sensory processing disorder: When the brain has trouble receiving and processing data sent by the senses.

Specific learning disability: A disorder that affects a person's ability to understand the various forms of a language resulting in challenges with thinking, reading, listening, writing, writing, or mathematical computations.

Speech impairment: A disorder that affects how a person verbally communicates

Stimulant medication: These are the most commonly recommended type of medication for ADHD. They act quickly to balance brain chemicals with limited side effects.

Systematic desensitization: Therapy used to make someone less sensitive to stimuli that typically trigger a negative response.

Target behavior: A specific behavior that one desires to increase or decrease.

Token economy system: A behavioral strategy that rewards children with tokens for displaying desired behavior. These tokens can be traded in for a larger reward once a certain amount has been collected.

Working memory: Short-term memory of the brain that processes information and helps manage your immediate thoughts, actions, and behavior (CHADD, n.d.b).

BIBLIOGRAPHY

ADDtitude Editors. (2022, April 11). *What I would never trade away.* ADDtitude. https://www.additudemag.com/slideshows/positives-of-adhd/

ADDtitude Editors. (2022, June 17). *ADHD statistics: New ADHD facts and research.* ADDtitude. https://www.additudemag.com/statistics-of-adhd/

ADHD Institute. (n.d.). *ADHD epidemiology.* https://adhd-institute.com/burden-of-adhd/epidemiology/

ADHD Institute. (n.d.). *Non-pharmacological therapy.* https://adhd-institute.com/disease-management/non-pharmacological-therapy/

ADHD parenting: Coaching and teaching your child on how to make friends. (2018, July 2). The ADHD Centre. https://www.adhdcentre.co.uk/adhd-parenting-coaching-teaching-your-child-on-how-to-make-friends/

The ADHD routine: How daily routine for kids with ADHD can be beneficial. (n.d.). CoordiKids. https://www.coordikids.com/the-adhd-routine/

Bertin, M. (2022, April 6). *Calm starts at home: How to teach emotional regulation skills.* ADDtitude. https://www.additudemag.com/emotional-regulation-skills-adhd-children/

Bhandari, S. (2021, March 21). *6 medical conditions similar to ADHD.* WebMD. https://www.webmd.com/add-adhd/childhood-adhd/medical-conditions-like-adhd

Brady, C. (2020, February 24). *My daughter is selfish and rude.* ADDtitude. https://www.additudemag.com/how-to-raise-a-caring-child/

Brown, T.E. (2022, July 2). *Exaggerated emotions: How and why ADHD triggers intense feelings.* ADDtitude. https://www.additudemag.com/slideshows/adhd-emotions-understanding-intense-feelings/

Brown, T. E. (n.d.). *ADHD and emotions.* Understood. https://www.understood.org/en/articles/adhd-and-emotions-what-you-need-to-know

Buzanko, C. (2021, March 18). *The key to ADHD emotional regulation? Cultivating gratitude, pride & compassion*. ADDtitude. https://www.additudemag.com/emotional-regulation-adhd-kids-strategies/

Carpenter, D. (2021, April 30). *Never punish a child for bad behaviour outside their control*. ADDtitude. https://www.additudemag.com/behavior-punishment-parenting-child-with-adhd/

CDC. (n.d.). *Symptoms and diagnosis of ADHD* https://www.cdc.gov/ncbddd/adhd/diagnosis.html

CDC. (n.d.). *Treatment of ADHD*. https://www.cdc.gov/ncbddd/adhd/treatment.html

CDC. (n.d.). *What is ADHD?* https://www.cdc.gov/ncbddd/adhd/facts.html#Causes

CHADD. (2017, November 30). *Helping children develop social skills*. https://chadd.org/adhd-weekly/helping-children-develop-social-skills/

CHADD. (n.d.a). *General prevalence of ADHD*. https://chadd.org/about-adhd/general-prevalence/

CHADD. (n.d.b). *Glossary of terms*. https://chadd.org/about-adhd/glossary-of-terms/

Coghill, D., Soutullo, C., d'Aubuisson, C. et al. (2008, October 28). *Impact of attention-deficit/hyperactivity disorder on the patient and family: Results from a European survey*. Child Adolescent Psychiatry Ment Health 2, 31 . https://doi.org/10.1186/1753-2000-2-31

Cohen, M. (2018, October 3). *Can you treat ADHD without drugs?* WebMD. https://www.webmd.com/add-adhd/childhood-adhd/can-you-treat-adhd-without-drugs

Cole, L. (2021, April 15). *76 famous successful people with ADHD*. MentalUP. https://www.mentalup.co/blog/famous-people-and-celebrities-with-adhd

Cronkelton, E. (2021, August 12). *What are the differences between an ADHD brain and a neurotypical brain*. Medical News Today. https://www.medicalnewstoday.com/articles/adhd-brain-vs-normal-brain#keydifferences

deBros, K., Willard, C., & Buck, E. (2022, April 4). *Free download: Kid-friendly mindful meditation exercises*. ADDtitude. https://www.addi

tudemag.com/download/mindfulness-for-adhd-kids-10-easy-meditation-exercises/?src=embed_link

Ditzel, J. (2022, May 18). *ADHD and emotions: Relationship and tips to manage.* Healthline. https://www.healthline.com/health/adhd/emotional-regulation#adhd-and-emotions

Edelman, G. (2022, March 7). *How to make friends: A guide for kids with ADHD (and their parents, too).* ADDtitude. https://www.additudemag.com/how-to-make-friends-a-guide-for-kids-with-adhd/

Flynn, L. (2022, January 23). *Behavioral parent training: Manage difficult ADHD behaviour.* ADDtitude. https://www.additudemag.com/adhd-behavior-therapy-parent-training-classes/

Gill, T. & Hosker, T. (2021, February 10). *ADHD may be impacting your child's social skills and what you can do to help.* Foothills Academy https://www.foothillsacademy.org/community/articles/adhd-social-skills

Gotter, A. & Burford, M. (2022, March 17). *Behavioral therapy: Definition, types & effectiveness.* Healthline. https://www.healthline.com/health/behavioral-therapy#techniques

The Healthline Editorial Team. (2021, April 16). *ADHD treatment options: Therapy, medication, and more.* Healthline. https://www.healthline.com/health/adhd/treatment-overview#1

Herskovitz, B. (2022, April 27). *Does my child have ADHD? 3 minute test & screening.* Psycom. https://www.psycom.net/does-my-child-have-adhd

Holland, K. (2018, July 23). *ADHD by the numbers: Facts, statistics and you.* Healthline https://www.healthline.com/health/adhd/facts-statistics-infographic#fast-facts

How can we help kids with self-regulation? (n.d.). Child Mind Institute. https://childmind.org/article/can-help-kids-self-regulation/

Jaksa, P. (2022, February 10). *The importance of a daily schedule for kids with ADHD: Sample routines and more.* ADDtitude. https://www.additudemag.com/sample-schedule-adhd-morning-after-school-bedtime/

Johns Hopkins Medicine. (n.d.). *Attention-deficit/Hyperactivity Disorder*

(ADHD) in children. https://www.hopkinsmedicine.org/health/conditions-and-diseases/adhdadd

Karen. (2019, September 4). *Why routine and structure are important for children who have ADHD.* Coastal Psychological Group. https://coastalpsychologicalgroup.com/2019/09/04/50820/

King, K., Alexander, D., & Seabi, J. (2016, June 3). *Siblings' perceptions of their ADHD diagnosed sibling's impact on the family system.* International Journal of Environmental Research and Public Health, 13(9), 910. https://doi.org/10.3390/ijerph13090910

Lori, Katie & Mallory (2021, October 18). *The truth about routines and ADHD.* The Childhood Collective. https://thechildhoodcollective.com/2021/10/18/the-truth-about-routines-and-adhd/

Low, K. (2020, June 29). *8 simple strategies for students with ADHD.* Verywell Mind. https://www.verywellmind.com/help-for-students-with-adhd-20538

Low, K. (2021, February 28). *How to improve social skills in children with ADHD.* Verywell Mind. https://www.verywellmind.com/how-to-improve-social-skills-in-children-with-adhd-20727

Low, K. (2022, April 19). *Why children with ADHD need structure and routines.* Verywell Mind. https://www.verywellmind.com/why-is-structure-important-for-kids-with-adhd-20747

Maguire, C. (2021, July 27). *Build back your child's social skills in 7 steps.* ADDtitude. https://www.additudemag.com/how-to-improve-social-skills-adhd-children/

Mayo Clinic Staff. (n.d.). *Attention-deficit/hyperactivity disorder (ADHD) in children—diagnosis and treatment.* Mayo Clinic. https://www.mayoclinic.org/diseases-conditions/adhd/diagnosis-treatment/drc-20350895

McNutt-English, A. & Peirce, A. (2021, July 13). *Moving ahead academically: 7 ways to help your child with ADHD in school.* Everyday Health https://www.everydayhealth.com/adhd/adhd-in-school.aspx

Miller, C. (n.d.). *What's ADHD (and what's not) in the classroom.* Child Mind Institute. https://childmind.org/article/whats-adhd-and-whats-not-in-the-classroom/

Morgan, P. L., Staff, J., Hillemeier, M. M., Farkas, G., & Maczuga, S.

(2013, July 1). *Racial and ethnic disparities in ADHD diagnosis from kindergarten to eighth grade.* Pediatrics, 132(1), 85–93. https://doi.org/10.1542/peds.2012-2390

Nall, R. (2021, January 19). *The benefits of ADHD.* Healthline. https://www.healthline.com/health/adhd/benefits-of-adhd#personality-strengths

NHS. (n.d.). *Attention deficit hyperactivity disorder (ADHD)—causes.* https://www.nhs.uk/conditions/attention-deficit-hyperactivity-disorder-adhd/causes/

NHS. (n.d.). *Diagnosis.* https://www.nhs.uk/conditions/attention-deficit-hyperactivity-disorder-adhd/diagnosis/

NHS. (n.d.). *Overview—attention deficit hyperactivity disorder.* https://www.nhs.uk/conditions/attention-deficit-hyperactivity-disorder-adhd/

Novik, L. (2021, June 9). *Parent's guide for disciplining kids who have ADHD.* Psych Central. https://psychcentral.com/adhd/parents-guide-for-disciplining-kids-with-adhd

Novotni, M. (2022, April 11). *Will our kids be okay?* https://www.additudemag.com/will-our-kids-be-ok/

Nutrition and exercise. (n.d.). Lanc UK. https://www.lanc.org.uk/nutrition-and-exercise/

Pedersen, T. (2022, February 15). *Can ADHD be cured? All you need to know.* Psychcentral. https://psychcentral.com/adhd/can-adhd-be-cured

Powell-Key, A. (2021, April 7). *ADHD in children: Managing moods and emotions.* WebMD. https://www.webmd.com/add-adhd/adhd-children-mood-swings

The power of gratitude: A magical tool for ADHD brains. (n.d.). ADDept. https://www.addept.org/living-with-adult-add-adhd/the-power-of-gratitude

Reber, D. (2022, April 30). *Accepting your child's ADHD diagnosis: How to embrace neurodiversity.* ADDtitude https://www.additudemag.com/neurodivergent-diagnosis-accept-your-child/

Segal, J. & Smith, M. (2021, October). *ADHD and school.* HelpGuide. https://www.helpguide.org/articles/add-adhd/attention-deficit-disorder-adhd-and-school.htm

7 benefits of cognitive behavioral therapy. (2015, February 16). Comprehensive Consultation Psychological Services. http://comprehendthemind.com/7-benefits-cognitive-behavioral-therapy/

Shaw, G. (2016, April 24). *Disciplining a child with ADHD.* WebMD. https://www.webmd.com/add-adhd/childhood-adhd/features/adhd-child-discipline

Sherrell, Z. (2021, July 20). *What are the benefits of ADHD?* Medical News Today. https://www.medicalnewstoday.com/articles/adhd-benefits#strengths-andbenefits

Silver, L. (2021, May 10). *The ADHD Brain: Neuroscience behind attention deficit disorder.* ADDtitude. https://www.additudemag.com/neuroscience-of-adhd-brain/

Sissons, B. (2019, June 28). *ADHD misdiagnosis: Why might it happen?* Medical News Today. https://www.medicalnewstoday.com/articles/325595

Smith, J. (2021, June 29). *ADHD and empathy: Identifying and resolving the disconnect.* FastBraiin. https://www.fastbraiin.com/blogs/blog/adhd-and-empathy

Smith, J. (2021, June 29). *How to implement a morning routine for your ADHD child.* FastBraiin. https://www.fastbraiin.com/blogs/blog/adhd-morning-routine

Tartakovsky, M. (2022, June 26). *10 strategies for helping kids with ADHD build self-confidence.* Psych Central. https://psychcentral.com/blog/10-strategies-for-helping-kids-with-adhd-build-self-confidence#

The Understood Team. (n.d.). *Download: Log to find out why your child gets frustrated.* Understood. https://www.understood.org/en/articles/download-frustration-log-to-find-out-why-your-child-gets-frustrated

Villines, Z. (2021, November 9). *The importance of ADHD awareness.* Medical News Today. https://www.medicalnewstoday.com/articles/adhd-awareness

Printed in Great Britain
by Amazon